MOUNTAIN BIKE FITNESS TRAINING

MOUNTAIN BIKE FITNESS TRAINING

John Metcalfe

MAINSTREAM
PUBLISHING
EDINBURGH AND LONDON

To my parents
for their unwavering support
and enthusiasm

First published in Great Britain in 2001 by
MAINSTREAM PUBLISHING COMPANY (EDINBURGH) LTD
7 Albany Street
Edinburgh EH1 3UG

ISBN 1 84018 424 8

A catalogue record for this book is available from the British Library

Typeset in Futurist and Stone
Printed and bound in Great Britain by
Creative Print and Design Wales

Acknowledgements

This book would not have been possible without the help of several key people. Thank you; you know who you are.

Contents

Preface

Mountain biking has come a long way since its inception back in the early '70s. Once considered an alternative form of recreation, it has undergone a renaissance period, and has emerged as an Olympic sport where the stars of mountain biking battle for top honours on the world stage. A lot has changed. Few of the current top riders can master every discipline of the sport, as was so often the case in yesteryear. No longer do the stars compete in the downhill, dual slalom, and trials on the Saturday, then race to glory in the cross-country on the Sunday.

Mountain bike equipment has evolved at such a pace that the bikes used in the various disciplines are as far removed from each other as a rally car is from a Formula-One racing car. A cross-country mountain bike would barely last a minute on the world downhill circuit, and a downhill steed would be totally unsuitable for a cross-country race.

Without a doubt mountain biking has become specialised, and has done so in a diminutive time-scale. Equipment has evolved that is specific to the task; and riders have been forced to specialise. It is no longer possible to be cycling fit, put in a hard ride, and have a fair chance of doing well. Each discipline has risen to a level where the fitness and intellectual demands placed on the competitors requires total dedication and application in training, with very little room for crossover.

A popular analogy in coaching circles equates matching the fitness of a rider to a specific discipline with matching a Lottery ticket to the winning numbers. Five numbers and the bonus will not win – only all six numbers bring you the top prize. Of course, the main difference with mountain bike fitness is that it is not all down to luck. You need hard work, dedication and an intelligent training programme to succeed.

This book is a compilation of modern mountain bike training theories and philosophies designed to enable you to construct your own training plan. The information that I offer in this book has evolved from sports science research, anecdotal evidence and personal experience. All these constructs are based on contemporary information and, by their very nature, they are transient and are subject to change and interpretation. Because this is a continually evolving project, I welcome any feedback and comments from you, the reader.

John Metcalfe, 2001

PART ONE

Introduction

1. FIT FOR WHAT?

– Definitions of fitness
– Components of mountain bike fitness
– Energy production

2. FITNESS ASSESSMENT AND GOAL-SETTING

– Identifying weak fitness areas
– The role of fitness testing
– Goal-setting

3. TRAINING PRINCIPLES

– Overload and supercompensation
– Progressive overload
– Over-training
– Specificity
– Reversibility
– Variety

1. FIT FOR WHAT?

DEFINITIONS OF FITNESS

The phrase 'I'm going to have to get fitter' gets used a lot during the mountain bike race season. This is especially so after a particularly gruelling race, or towards the end of a race series when most riders have been put through their paces. We have all used the phrase ourselves at one time or another, but what exactly do we mean by getting fitter? And, more importantly, how do you go about getting fit?

Well, fitness can be a very intractable term to define because it is intricately woven into the fabric of our everyday speech. Fitness has multiple meanings, ranging from the widespread understanding of being in suitable condition to perform a task, to a more depressing clinical interpretation of being defined as a distance from death.

Even putting these mainstream definitions aside, within the sport of mountain biking there is much contention about the understanding of the concept. Different riders have different interpretations. What an Expert class rider regards as fitness differs greatly from that of a Fun class rider (see chapter seventeen). But on the whole, getting fit boils down to the same thing: being able to ride faster for longer.

For the purpose of this book, I shall apply the sports science interpretation of the term fitness, and will focus mainly upon the physical and skill-related properties of a rider. The components of fitness that are required in mountain biking are summarised in table 1. However, the mental fitness of a rider can often be the determining factor between racing success and failure because it orchestrates all of the other fitness components. It is important that we have an understanding of each of these components and what its specific role in mountain biking is.

Table 1: Components of Mountain Bike Fitness

PHYSICAL		SKILL
Strength	Aerobic Power	Agility
Speed	Flexibility	Co-ordination
Anaerobic Power	Body Composition	Balance
Muscular Endurance		Reaction Time

COMPONENTS OF MOUNTAIN BIKE FITNESS

Physical Fitness

When riders talk about having to get fit, it is usually the physical aspects of fitness that they are referring to. This is the area of fitness that most mountain bikers associate with improved performance, and the individual components that comprise physical fitness are discussed below.

STRENGTH Scientifically speaking, strength is the ability of a muscle, or a group of muscles, to generate a force against a resistance. Maximal, or absolute, strength refers to the maximum amount of force a muscle can exert over a short period of time. Whilst this may be of major importance in weight lifting, it is rarely a factor in mountain biking. Of greater relevance to your mountain bike performance is your ability to generate dynamic strength. Dynamic strength is concerned with being strong over a prolonged period of time. The peak force that is generated is considerably less than that during a maximal strength exertion, but it can be sustained for longer. You will be calling on your dynamic strength when you are sprinting for the holeshot, or are cranking your way up a steep climb.

SPEED In its literal sense, the speed component of your fitness is concerned with the rate at which you are able to complete the distance of the course. The quicker the time it takes you, the faster you are. However, speed is also related to how quickly you can set your limbs in motion. If you have a fast leg speed you will be able to generate high cadences, which in turn will also be a determining factor in your ability to accelerate quickly.

ANAEROBIC POWER Anaerobic power is the maximum rate at which you can generate energy from your anaerobic systems. In mountain biking, anaerobic power is used to sustain highly intense activity such as the starting sprint, or it can be used in explosive movements such as jumps and bunny hops. Downhill mountain biking and dual slalom require a high degree of anaerobic power.

MUSCULAR ENDURANCE Muscular endurance is the capacity of a muscle to contract repeatedly without fatiguing. In order to turn the cranks continually throughout a cross-country race, you will need a high degree of muscular endurance.

AEROBIC POWER Aerobic power (often called aerobic work capacity) is the rate at which you can produce energy from your aerobic energy system. As the name suggests, aerobic power requires the presence of oxygen, and is highly dependent on the efficiency of your cardiovascular system. If this component is highly developed you will be able to maintain a fast pace for a prolonged period of time without lactic acid accumulating.

FLEXIBILITY Flexibility is concerned with the range of movement in a joint. Upon first appraisal the role of flexibility in mountain biking may appear to be limited – and as such it is often overlooked – this is not the case. Flexibility, as we shall see in subsequent chapters, is a significant mountain bike fitness component and can contribute greatly to the efficiency and safety of a rider.

BODY COMPOSITION Body composition refers to the relative percentages of body fat and lean muscle tissue. To enhance your cycling efficiency, you should aim to maximise your lean tissue whilst minimising your body fat.

Skill-Related Fitness

Skill-related fitness is an area often overlooked when fitness training is discussed colloquially. However, the skill components are a legitimate aspect of mountain bike fitness. After all, there is no point being super fit in a physical sense if you can't ride your mountain bike efficiently.

AGILITY Agility is a product of co-ordination, balance and reaction time. It is concerned with being able to alter the position of your body very quickly and accurately without losing your balance. All mountain bike disciplines require this component to a high degree, but none more so than dual slalom, where obstacles and other riders must be avoided.

CO-ORDINATION Co-ordination in mountain biking is concerned with being able to orchestrate each of your body parts in order to produce accurate, flawless skills. For some lucky riders co-ordination seems to be innate; fortunately, for those other mere mortals, co-ordination can be learnt and improved with practice.

BALANCE In its simplest sense, balance is about being able to stay on two wheels without falling over. As a mountain biker, your ability to balance is aided greatly by your momentum and the gyroscopic effects of your wheels. In other words if you ride fast you'll have a greater chance of staying upright. However, this is not the complete story because a large amount of skill is also required in order to maintain a stable position, especially when you are riding slowly or on undulating terrain.

REACTION TIME Reaction time is concerned with how quickly you respond to a stimulus. In mountain biking there many stimuli to respond to – trees, roots, rocks and other riders, to name but a few. Each one of these stimuli has many possible responses and, as such, choices have to made. Therefore reaction time also involves decision making, and this has been found to be greatly influenced by experience.

It follows that in order to 'get fit' each one of your fitness components must be enhanced and honed to the extent that it matches the fitness requirements of your chosen mountain bike discipline. No matter how advanced some of your fitness components are, you will only be as good as your weakest component, so the process of getting fit is a juggling act where you must continually keep working on every aspect of your fitness. Unfortunately, this process of improvement cannot go on indefinitely. Each of us has a predetermined, maximum level for each component as determined by our genes. To reach your genetic potential is an arduous task to say the least, and as you strive to improve your mountain bike fitness you will be continually hampered by other constraining factors. Your main adversary is going to be your ability to produce energy.

ENERGY PRODUCTION

Even if you have reached the envious condition of having all of your fitness components harmoniously operating at their ceiling limits, all is not done. Your body's systems need energy to function properly: no matter how well developed they are, if they don't get the correct amount of energy at the appropriate time they will grind to a halt. Ultimately the energy used to fuel these systems comes from the food that you eat, and your ability to extract the chemical energy from food can determine how well you are going to race. It really can be as simple as that.

The nutrient energy 'locked up' in your food cannot be used directly by your working muscles. Instead it must be converted, by a chemical process called respiration, to adenosine triphosphate (ATP). This comprises an adenosine molecule with three phosphates attached to it via energy-rich bonds. The energy released when these bonds are broken is then used to power the muscular contractions that you make. Humans are only able to store a limited amount of ATP, and as such it can only supply the energy for a few seconds of physical activity. Therefore ATP must be continually re-synthesised.

There are three ways that your body can continually re-synthesise ATP whilst you are exercising, these are:

PHOSPHOCREATINE SYSTEM The muscles also store phosphocreatine (PC) which is another chemical compound with energy rich bonds. The energy yielded when PC is metabolised is used to re-synthesise ATP. Once again the stores of PC are also limited and can only contribute about another three to four seconds of physical activity before becoming depleted. Obviously mountain bike races last longer than several seconds, so your body will switch to another system to produce energy – anaerobic glycolysis.

ANAEROBIC GLYCOLYSIS Anaerobic glycolysis is the process whereby nutrient energy from the metabolism of carbohydrates is used to re-synthesise ATP. In order to yield energy relatively quickly, this process is performed anaerobically (without oxygen). As a result the carbohydrate is not fully metabolised and lactic acid is the by-product. Every mountain biker should be familiar with the sensations associated with lactic acid accumulation; it is that burning feeling in your thighs just after you have done a hard sprint. Anaerobic glycolysis contributes to the energy equation for relatively intense exercise lasting several minutes, for example when you attempt to lose a competitor by increasing the pace for several minutes.

If your mountain biking is to continue for longer than several minutes, your body will produce energy from the final system – aerobic glycolysis.

AEROBIC GLYCOLYSIS Aerobic glycolysis involves the complete metabolism of food and requires the presence of oxygen. The maximum amount of energy is released and there is no lactic acid produced. The price of this efficiency is a slower energy turnover than that of anaerobic glycolysis. Because of this, if you wish to ride for long periods, you must accommodate a reduction in your pace. Aerobic glycolysis is a significant contributor of energy when you are competing in a cross country race, and it is also the energy system of choice in ultra-distance events and expedition touring.

It is therefore the availability of both oxygen and substrate (fuel) to the working muscles that is the major limiting factor in your ability to produce energy. If there is not enough oxygen present and lactic acid is allowed to accumulate in your muscles you will fatigue prematurely and your performance will suffer. This occurs when you sprint as fast as you can, for example at the start of a race. Here you will be exercising anaerobically, and as you know you cannot keep this pace up for very long. Pretty soon you have two options: either slow down the pace so that you can meet your body's oxygen demands, or continue at this pace for a short while and then grind to a complete halt.

The solution is not just a case of breathing in more air, absorbing more oxygen and therefore getting fitter. Instead there is a long chain of events that occur between your breathing in air, and oxygen arriving at your exercising leg muscles. As you inhale, air is drawn into the lungs. Then, during the process of gaseous exchange, oxygen has to combine with your red blood cells. The blood is then pumped to your working muscles by your heart and thence through the body. The oxygen from the blood then has to be extracted by the working muscles. Oxygen absorption and utilisation is thus dependent upon the efficiency of your lungs, the ability of your blood to carry oxygen, the ability of your heart to pump the blood, and the efficiency of your muscle fibres.

The maximum volume of oxygen that you are able to absorb and use is called your VO_2 max. It is measured in ml/kg of bodyweight/minute. In mountain biking circles, this value has become synonymous with fitness: if rider A has a greater VO_2 maximum than rider B, Rider A is often considered to be the fitter. But as we shall see in subsequent chapters, this is a misconception because VO_2 max is really only a measure of your fitness potential.

It follows that a deficiency in any of the many links in the above chain will drastically reduce your potential capacity to produce energy. It is apparent that a number of the constricting factors are beyond your control, and you can therefore do little about them. What you can do, however, is aim to accentuate each of the links that you can influence, and the only vehicle that can help you achieve this goal is the appropriate type of training.

2. FITNESS ASSESSMENT
AND GOAL-SETTING

IDENTIFYING WEAK FITNESS AREAS

If we examine the riding abilities of any mountain bike champion we can see that they have no weak areas – just strong ones. This is because mountain bike performance is the result of an elaborate chain of fitness components that all act together synergistically. Your overall mountain bike performance is not just the sum of these separate abilities. In the same way that a chain is only as strong as its weakest link, you are only as good as your worst ability.

Research has shown that, when left to their own devices, most athletes avoid training their weak areas because they are no good at them. Instead, human nature being what it is, they train their strong areas because it makes them feel good. The net result is that their strengths get stronger and their weaknesses weaker. Unfortunately, one does not necessarily offset the other. For example, if your forte is climbing, then being extra good at climbing is not going to make up for poor endurance in a race. You simply will not last the course. In this instance, you would be better off focusing your efforts on bringing your weak link up to par.

Small changes in your weak areas will have a great effect on your overall performance, while making a significant improvement in your strongest areas will have a diminished effect. Therefore when devising your training programme, you must first of all identify your weakest areas and make them your number-one training priority. Focusing on your weaknesses is not a negative approach. Once you have highlighted your troublesome fitness components, it is like discovering that you have been driving around with your handbrake on. Once you've realised this, you can release the brake that has blighted your progress, and reap the benefits.

Identifying, learning about and monitoring your weak points is half the battle in mountain bike training. Before you begin to design your mountain bike training programme, it is imperative that you have your fitness level assessed. Fitness assessment tests are an integral part of any mountain bike training plan, as they allow a snapshot of your fitness status at a particular point in time. Pre-training fitness tests give you an overview of your initial fitness level, which, if compared to the fitness demands of the sport, will highlight your weak areas. You can then use this information to design your yearly training programme.

Diagram 1 illustrates a hypothetical situation where a rider has undergone several tests to assess the status of a number of fitness components. Clearly components A and C are weak areas and require attention, whereas component B is a strong area and should be maintained.

Diagram 1: Comparing Desired and Actual Fitness Levels

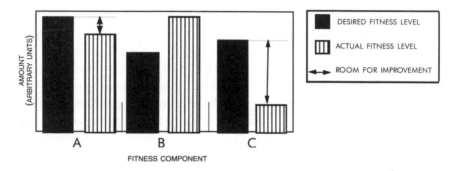

THE ROLE OF FITNESS TESTING

In order to ascertain the fitness demands of mountain biking you need to analyse the fitness components of riders who are better than you. If you are nearing the upper echelons of mountain biking, it would be useful for you to obtain fitness data for professional riders. This is often a lot easier said than done, as data like this is usually a closely guarded secret. An alternative approach is to contact the British Cycling Federation (BCF) and ask for a copy of their selection criteria for fitness tests. You can then use this as a yardstick and see how you measure up. If, however, you have not yet reached such dizzy heights in your mountain bike career, a more practical approach would be to assess those riders who are performing well in your race category. Once again, you may find that riders are a bit cagey about broadcasting their fitness data because they don't want to give anything away. However, if you are a member of a good mountain bike club, the more experienced riders are often more than willing to lend a helpful hand and share whatever information you need.

Testing also serves an important role during your training programme, as it provides you with valuable feedback about how you are progressing (or, just as importantly, if you're not). If you are on course then this confirmation is an all-important confidence boost. If your training is not going as planned, the test results will highlight which areas in your training programme need altering in order to bring about the desired effect.

Fitness testing need not mean white coats and laboratories. In fact, anything you use to assess your fitness can be classified as a test. For example, you may perform a ten-mile time trial as part of your training, or enter the same race each month, and compare the results over time to see if you are getting any better. This anecdotal approach is fine for getting a 'feel' for how things are going; but can you be sure that the reason why you got a better result this time was due to an increased fitness and not because there was a tailwind this week? Or because less people turned up for the race this month? You must also be sure that you know exactly which aspect of your fitness you are trying to assess.

For this reason it is best to use validated and reliable tests rather than make up your own. Without a doubt the most accurate fitness tests are those performed in laboratories, but what they gain in accuracy they can lose on sport specificity. They can also be expensive and inconvenient. It is possible to get a free laboratory assessment by contacting your local university Exercise Physiology department and offering your services as a guinea pig. Exercise Physiology undergraduates are always looking for subjects to test and will no doubt be glad of your call.

A compromise between accuracy and sports specificity does exist. Field-test equivalents of the laboratory tests have been designed which have the best of both worlds: they are sport specific whilst maintaining a good degree of accuracy. Throughout this book, where appropriate, I have included the relevant testing protocols.

You should ensure that you perform your fitness tests under similar conditions every time (same venue, weather conditions, time of day, etc.) as this will reduce the number of uncontrollable variables and render your tests more accurate. Also try to make things equal within yourself by ensuring you get enough rest, and that you have adequate glycogen stores for the tests.

Due to their nature, fitness tests are physically demanding and as such care must be taken to ensure that they do not detract from your training. Use them sparingly and substitute them with the corresponding workout in order to avoid over-training. The proof is in the pudding, as they say, and a great deal of information about your weak areas can be gleaned from a post-race analysis. Below is a questionnaire, based on a Likert scale, which you should complete after each race. The results from this should be in accordance with your physical fitness tests, but they may also unearth other weaknesses that are not always apparent until you are put in a race scenario.

By definition you cannot have weak spots in all areas. You may have one or two areas holding you back which are relatively weak compared to your other abilities. Concentrate on making these weaknesses your future strengths. Be smart: work on these areas until you feel your efforts would gain greater results if you applied them to another aspect of your mountain biking training.

Table 2: Fitness Assessment Questionnaire

SCORING THE QUESTIONNAIRE:

Rate your ability in each category on the corresponding scale using the following key:

5 – strongly agree

4 – agree

3 – neutral

2 – disagree

1 – strongly disagree

Compute the scores for each component. The range for each component is from 4 (very weak) to 20 (very strong) with the average being 12. Rate each of the components to assess your strong and weak areas.

VERY WEAK		WEAK			BELOW AVERAGE		AVERAGE		ABOVE AVERAGE		STRONG			VERY STRONG	
4	5	6	7	8	9	10	11	12	13	14	15	16	17	18	19	20

COMPONENT: ANAEROBIC THRESHOLD / LACTATE TOLERANCE

During the race . . .

When I performed repeated sprints, my last sprint was as good as my first	— 5 — 4 — 3 — 2 — 1 —
I recovered quickly after sprinting hard	— 5 — 4 — 3 — 2 — 1 —
I regularly out-sprinted other riders	— 5 — 4 — 3 — 2 — 1 —
When I was sprinting 'all out' my pace was constant and didn't taper off	— 5 — 4 — 3 — 2 — 1 —

COMPONENT: ENDURANCE

During the race . . .

I perform better than if it were run over a shorter distance	— 5 — 4 — 3 — 2 — 1 —
I overtook more people during the latter part of the race than overtook me	— 5 — 4 — 3 — 2 — 1 —
I did not feel daunted by the length of the race	— 5 — 4 — 3 — 2 — 1 —
I did not feel weak towards the end	— 5 — 4 — 3 — 2 — 1 —

COMPONENT: CLIMBING (CROSS-COUNTRY SPECIFIC)

During the race . . .

I overtook more people on the climbs than overtook me	— 5 — 4 — 3 — 2 — 1 —
I recovered quickly after climbing hard	— 5 — 4 — 3 — 2 — 1 —
I performed best on the climbs	— 5 — 4 — 3 — 2 — 1 —
On longer climbs, my pace is constant and doesn't taper off	— 5 — 4 — 3 — 2 — 1 —

COMPONENT: POWER

During the race . . .

I was with the leaders at the start	— 5 — 4 — 3 — 2 — 1 —
I recover quickly after explosive hard sprints	— 5 — 4 — 3 — 2 — 1 —
I was able to 'honk' up short steep hills	— 5 — 4 — 3 — 2 — 1 —
I was able to drop riders over short distances	— 5 — 4 — 3 — 2 — 1 —

COMPONENT: SKILLS/ERGONOMICS

During the race . . .

I made very few gear selection errors	— 5 — 4 — 3 — 2 — 1 —
I did not fall off very often	— 5 — 4 — 3 — 2 — 1 —
I was faster on the tight tricky single track than most other riders	— 5 — 4 — 3 — 2 — 1 —
I enjoyed the tight turns, drop-offs, and negotiating obstacles	— 5 — 4 — 3 — 2 — 1 —

GOAL-SETTING

The road to fitness can be an undulating one, littered with numerous blind alleys and cul-de-sacs. But as with any journey, life is made far easier with a clearly defined destination and a map showing the quickest possible way to get there. Despite the well-documented advantages of having a game plan to adhere to, anecdotal evidence suggests that very few mountain bikers actually have a tangible goal that they can work towards. This lack of direction invariably leads to a 'hit-and-miss' approach to training and results in a lot of misguided time and effort.

If you have followed the above advice and have identified your weak links, then you are halfway to setting yourself appropriate training goals. But, before you put any physical effort into your mountain bike training, it is wise to assess exactly what it is you want to achieve, and clearly define your goals. Sports psychology research suggests a set of criteria that a goal must meet in order for it to be fully effective. The criteria are as follows:

Specific
Your goals must be clearly defined. This single factor cannot be overstated. You should know exactly what it is you are working towards; preferably you should also include a realistic timescale. Just wanting to get fitter, or win a race is too nebulous. Your goals need to be tangible. Wanting to lose two kilograms of bodyweight within a month is an example of a specific goal.

Improvement
To be worthwhile, your fitness goals should be based on continual improvement, rather than just maintaining your current performance.

Controllable
It is important that you have control over your goals if they are to be effective. Wanting to beat another rider is not a controllable goal; it is outcome orientated, greatly influenced by the other rider. Even if you were to attain this goal, you have no way of knowing whether it was due to your increased fitness levels or whether the other rider just had a bad race. Of course, success in mountain bike racing is all about being victorious, and no doubt your principal goal will be to attain a certain ranking in relation to other riders. This is fine, but you must also ensure that your fitness goals along the way are controllable and relevant to you. Make them performance related.

Challenging
Setting yourself an easy goal will give you very little reward and satisfaction. Similarly, unrealistic, difficult goals will be the cause of much aggravation. You should therefore set yourself practical goals which are a challenge to achieve.

Attainable
It follows then that your goals must be attainable. If you set yourself the sole task of winning the World Championships before you have even won a Sports class (see chapter seventeen) race, then it will no doubt be the cause of much disappointment. It is fine to want to climb to the summit of Everest; just be sure to make base camps on the way up. Make your goals as difficult as possible, yet attainable with effort.

Measurable
It is important that you have some way of measuring whether or not you have been

successful at achieving your goal. You must therefore have clearly defined objectives from the outset. Just wanting to be fitter is not a measurable goal, for you need to state quantitatively the level of fitness that you wish to achieve. Fitness diagnostic tests are excellent tools for measuring your goals.

Personal

Your goals must be specific to you. You should set yourself personal goals that are not unduly influenced by the performance of others. You should also bear in mind that, longitudinally, your goals are transient and will change. Your goals for now will no doubt change over time as you successively attain them.

It is also a good idea to stratify your goals in to three levels, as highlighted below:

Level I

These are the goals that you should be able to achieve. Here you might include the basic fitness level that you should be able to reach unless something goes awry.

Level II

These are the goals that you could achieve it you truly worked at them. These are your main goals that are attainable with effort. If you have more than one goal then you should prioritise them.

Level III

These are the goals that are possible, and that you just might achieve if everything goes your way. Don't make these unrealistic – remember, they must still be possible.

Once you have decided upon your goals, write them down. This is a big step. Your goals have now changed from an abstract idea to something that is tangible. For the first time, you now have evidence of the mountain bike goals that you wish to achieve. Your next step is to set yourself a realistic timescale for achieving them. Again, be specific and write down the actual date. For your primary mountain bike goal this date will probably be synonymous with the date of your most important race. However you should also include timescales for your other goals. To complete the goal-setting procedure, you should also write down a plan of how you are going to achieve them. This final step is dealt with in greater detail in chapter eight.

As you can see, the philosophy behind goal-setting is that it is a dynamic and ever-changing process: what is a goal now may need to be modified in a month or two when you achieve it. In order to keep progressing, you must constantly assess your abilities and alter your goals accordingly.

3. TRAINING PRINCIPLES

OVERLOAD AND SUPERCOMPENSATION

Now that you have established your weak areas and clearly defined your training goals, the next step is to apply the principles of training. The basic concept behind any training programme is to make your body perform more exercise than it is accustomed to. For mountain biking this involves riding further (duration), more often (frequency), or faster (intensity) than normal, or a combination of all three. Increasing the exercise like this is termed 'overload'. Overloading in this manner puts greater stress on your body than usual and causes your metabolic and biological systems to work at maximal or near maximal efforts.

As a result of overload your body upgrades, or adapts, to the new workload and becomes more efficient. When this adaptation has occurred, the exercise is said to have initiated a training response. Sports scientists call this upgrading 'supercompensation' (A in diagram 2), and it allows you to perform more work for the same amount of effort, or the same work with less effort. Put another way: you have become fitter.

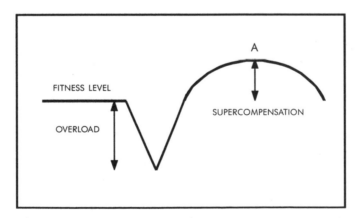

Diagram 2: Overload and Supercompensation

PROGRESSIVE OVERLOAD

If you so wished you could leave it there and rest on your laurels; however, a properly designed mountain bike programme will incorporate progressive overload. Progressive overload is the same principle as overload, except that at the peak of supercompensation you should increase the workload again, which causes further adaptation. This should continue until you reach your maximum mountain bike potential. In theory it sounds easy, but in practice it can be a different story.

Diagram 3: Progressive Overload

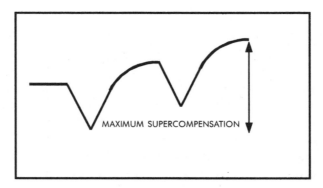

MAXIMUM SUPERCOMPENSATION

Diagrammatically, progressive overload is an easy concept to understand. However, when it comes to transferring the principle to a real-life training situation, problems arise. The issue is not with the progressive overload principle per se, but how it is used and applied. People think, 'If this much exercise is making me this much fitter, then twice as much exercise will make me twice as fit, right?' WRONG!

Your body does not get fit when you are riding your mountain bike. In fact it only supercompensates or adapts when you are resting, so recovery periods should be built into every mountain bike training programme. If you regularly overload your body and do not allow time for adequate recovery and adaptation to occur, you are running the risk of over-training.

OVER-TRAINING

Over-training is a widely used term and is all too often used generically to explain poor performance. There are in fact two precursor conditions before a state of over-training is actually reached.

The first stage is called 'overload' as described above. If insufficient rest occurs, it is quickly followed by the second stage, which is termed 'over-reaching'. Characteristic symptoms of over-reaching are a noticeable deterioration in your mountain bike performance, and a persistent feeling that you are not operating at 100 per cent. These symptoms are sometimes hard to detect – riders can easily shrug them off, just thinking they are having a 'bad week' – but once they are recognised, a return to form is possible following a few days of complete rest. Unfortunately the typical knee-jerk reaction to these symptoms is the belief that more training will kick-start the training progression. Of course this just stirs up the muddied waters and facilitates the onset of the full-blown condition of over-training.

Diagram 4: Over-training

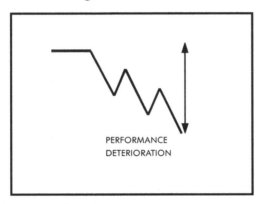

PERFORMANCE
DETERIORATION

The problem is not knowing when you are at the height of supercompensation, and therefore when you should start your subsequent exercise bout. Initiate your next workout after supercompensation has occurred and you will not be improving your fitness at your optimal rate. Initiate it too early and you run the risk of over-training. It is a fine line that you have to tread, and the only way to learn is through experience, trial and error, and careful monitoring of your recovery status.

Both mentally and physically, over-training is a severe form of fatigue, with the only cure being complete rest. Ironically, the condition is brought about by the same three factors that improve performance: training for too long, training too often, or training too hard. Nine times out of ten, it is the latter situation that leads to over-training in mountain bikers. This is because a lot of mountain bikers don't know how to 'train easy'. As you shall see later in this book, easy training days are an integral component of a mountain biker's training programme. Easy days – or active recovery days, as they are known – are necessary in order to facilitate the recovery process. When performing training at this easy intensity, a lot of riders fall into the trap of thinking that it is of no benefit to them, and if they are to salvage anything from the workout then they are going to have to up the ante. This is a recipe for disaster. With an increase in intensity, and a subsequent reduction in recovery, over-training is a certainty.

Because there is such a fine line between maximal improvement and over-training, a lot of mountain bikers are over-trained. Typical indications of over-training include: a lack of improvement in mountain bike performance despite continued training; a lack of appetite; insomnia; elevated morning heart rate; general lethargy; persistent colds; lingering muscle soreness; poor concentration; and a lack of motivation.

To make things difficult, it is quite normal for any one of these symptoms to be present during a non-over-trained period without requiring cause for concern. What you must be alert for is the continued presence of a combination of these ailments, or a continuous change in your normal condition. As a rule of thumb, if you suspect you are over-training, back off for a few days and see if your energy, motivation and performance improve. If they do, take a further week off training (more if necessary) in order to complete the recovery process fully, and when you return to your training keep a keen eye on your recovery status. Remember: if in doubt, rest.

SPECIFICITY

The specificity principle refers to the particular biological effects that a certain method of training has. It follows, then, that sprint training initiates certain adaptations which are different from those brought about by long-distance rides and vice versa. Similarly, a weight-training programme for your legs will not increase the muscle bulk of your arms. This may sound like common sense, but there are an awful lot of riders who go out on a 'training ride' not knowing exactly what it is they are working on.

The point to bear in mind when you are designing your training programme is that training is not a 'hit-and-miss' affair; you can't just go out for a ride and get fit. Because specific training methods initiate specific training changes, you should know exactly what fitness component you are targeting and then train accordingly.

REVERSIBILITY

The dictum 'if you don't use it, you'll lose it' underpins the reversibility principle. De-training occurs when the training adaptations are reversed or lost due to a period of reduced training or inactivity. Research has shown that significant decreases occur after only one or two weeks' inactivity. This reversal is an in-built primal function that has evolved over the millennia to ensure that our bodies are thrifty and operate at their most economical level. From a survival perspective, there is no point servicing and maintaining extra tissues if they are not needed; they are a waste of precious resources. So in order to get fit and build new tissue, we must justify their existence through hard training.

The important ramifications of this principle are that training changes are therefore transient and reversible. This means that you must still train, even if you only want to maintain your fitness, and the fitter you get the harder it becomes to initiate a training response.

VARIETY

The bottom line is that boredom kills training. It is the major reason why riders quit training programmes. No matter how motivated you are, if the training programme is repetitive and uninteresting then your enthusiasm will wane and your fitness level will stagnate or even deteriorate. You should enjoy your training and actually look forward to it. If you find yourself dreading the next workout, or trying to find excuses as to why you cannot train, something is wrong with your programme. It is time for a change.

PART TWO

Mountain Bike Training

4. EQUIPMENT, WARM-UP AND RECOVERY

- Appraisal of equipment required
- The warm-up
- The role of recovery

5. FLEXIBILITY

- Benefits of flexibility
- Stretching methods
- Stretching programme

6. STRENGTH TRAINING

- The theory of strength training
- Strength training tips
- Strength training programme
- Alternative strength training methods

7. FURTHER TRAINING METHODS

- Heart-rate training zones
- Anaerobic threshold training
- Interval training

- Fartlek training
- Aerobic endurance
- Plyometric training

8. PUTTING IT ALL TOGETHER

- The theory of periodisation and scheduling
- Phases making up the training year
- Year-round racing
- Training camps
- Training errors
- Being your own training coach
- Monitoring your performance

9. SPECIAL GROUPS

- Youth riders
- Junior riders
- Masters/veterans
- Female mountain bikers
- Ultra-endurance/adventure bikers
- Mountain bike tourers
- Fitness mountain bikers

10. ALTERNATIVE FORMS OF TRAINING

- The theory of cross-training
- Road cycling
- Running
- Hiking
- Swimming
- Other sports

– Muscle cramp

– Backache

– Delayed onset of muscle soreness

– Knee pain

– Nausea, dizziness and lethargy

– Masking medication

4. EQUIPMENT, WARM-UP
AND RECOVERY

APPRAISAL OF EQUIPMENT REQUIRED

Part two of this book outlines how to maximise your fitness components and match them to the discipline of your choice. Because the components of fitness form the 'nuts and bolts' of any athletic training programme, the following workouts are relevant to all mountain bike categories. What does differ between disciplines is the contribution each workout makes to the overall programme. The obvious example is that every type of rider needs some degree of endurance, but it is the cross-country rider who will focus on it the most.

The workouts described in this part of the book are what you will be doing on a day-to-day basis. The application you put in here will have a snowball effect on your overall fitness level. Get it right from the start and you will reap the benefits later on. Conversely, there is the potential to go off at a tangent, blissfully unaware of any errors that are being made. Fortunately there are several types of equipment on the market that will enable you to keep a tight rein on your training, and ensure that you are doing exactly what you are supposed to be doing. Listed below are several essential items of equipment that serious mountain bike racers should have in their fitness toolbox in order to maximise training efficiency.

Heart-rate Monitor

Intensity of effort is probably the single most important factor in your mountain bike training, yet it is the most difficult to gauge subjectively. The intensity at which your heart is working ultimately determines which aspect of your fitness you develop. With the advent of the heart-rate monitor in the early 1980s, mountain bike training has taken on a more scientific approach and has never looked back.

In its basic form, a heart-rate monitor is a two-part device: a transmitter belt that sits just below your chest; and a watch-style receiver. The transmitter picks up the electrical impulses that accompany your heartbeat and sends this information wirelessly to the receiver, which displays the heart rate numerically. A heart-rate monitor can be viewed as being similar to a rev counter in a car. Just as a rev counter informs you how hard the engine is working, a heart-rate monitor tells you how hard you are working, thus removing any subjectivity.

Once the preserve of the sponsored rider, heart-rate monitors are now more accessible to the private racer. This is due mainly to the dramatic drop in cost. There are many types of heart-rate monitor on the market today, with manufacturers bringing out new models all of the time. The basic heart-rate monitors that have the sole function of representing your heart rate are adequate for your training and can easily be attached to your handlebar by fastening it to a small section of pipe insulation. These models are within the budget of most riders (£50 to £60). However, as more features are added, the cost rises quite considerably. Mid-range features include limit settings, timers, and memory recall. At the top end of the range are computer-compatible heart-rate monitors which allow you to download all your training data via an interface and save it as a file on your computer for analysis at a later stage. In addition, manufacturers such as Polar produce cycle specific heart-rate monitors which include all the functions of a heart-rate monitor plus those of a cycle computer, with added options such as cadence and altitude.

Table 3: Summary of Heart-rate Monitor Functions

FUNCTION	DESCRIPTION
HEART RATE	This tells you how hard your heart is working. Good quality training can be performed with just this information.
AVERAGE HEART RATE	During a mountain bike race, for example, your heart rate will fluctuate widely. It will soar on the climbs but will drop when you are coasting. It can often be difficult to ascertain what the average intensity of the ride was. Some heart-rate monitors have the facility to compute the average heart rate.
TRAINING ZONES	This allows you to set the limits of your training zone. If your exercise intensity falls outside your target zone, a warning alarm will sound or the display will blink.
MEMORY	This allows for heart-rate information to be stored and viewed at a later date. It is often difficult to keep an eye on your heart-rate monitor whilst navigating difficult terrain. This function allows you to recall the information for later analysis.
CALORIE COUNTER	Calculates how many calories you have used during the exercise. A good function if you are concerned about weight control.

CYCLE FUNCTIONS
Some models incorporate the usual cycle computer functions into the heart-rate monitor. They are usually supplied with a handlebar mounting system which enables easy viewing and operation whilst you are on the move.

MULTI-LINE DISPLAY
This allows you to view several displays at once. It is essential if you are performing intervals or are involved in a timed event such as a Polaris or Trailquest where it is important to know the elapsed time as well as your heart rate.

WATCH FUNCTIONS
Enables you to use your heart-rate monitor as an everyday watch.

PC COMPATIBILITY
This is the function that really hikes up the price. It enables you to download the information to your PC and monitor your progress over time. A great function if you can afford it, but is really only necessary for the professional rider or coach.

THE ROLE OF THE HEART-RATE MONITOR The role of the heart-rate monitor is to supplement your training and supply you with additional information which can help you structure your training for maximum effect. It is therefore only a training tool and not a dictator. Many riders often become a slave to their heart-rate monitors and train religiously according to prescribed heart-rate training zones. However this is not always the best approach. Sometimes you may need a rest when your heart rate indicates that you don't, or vice versa.

Heart-rate training tends to split the competitive mountain bike fraternity in two: those who favour it and those who don't. What does become apparent, though, is that the higher you go in terms of level of competition, the more the riders use heart-rate monitors as part of their training. Yes, it may detract from the freedom of mountain biking, but it also keeps a tight rein on your training and can help direct it towards your goals.

CALCULATING MAXIMUM AND MINIMUM HEART RATE In subsequent chapters we shall apply heart-rate training zones to practical workouts. This allows you to tailor your training to suit your own physiology. In order to do this you will need to find out your maximum (Hr max) and minimum (Hr min) heart rates.

The best way to determine your maximum heart rate is by performing a ramped maximal test in a sports science laboratory under medical supervision.

By its very nature the test is maximal and places a lot of strain on the body. It is possible to perform a field-test version to determine maximum heart rate, but it is imperative that there is someone there to supervise you. If you are in any doubt about your ability to exercise maximally you should consult your doctor prior to attempting the test.

For this test you will need a long hill (about 5 km) that will allow you to ride up it for about 5 minutes. With your heart rate monitor on, attack the hill at race speed. Maintain this pace until you are about 1.5 km from the top and then sprint maximally to the finish. You should attain your maximum heart rate at the top.

To calculate your minimum heart rate is a lot easier. Upon waking in the morning, put on your heart-rate monitor and lie comfortably for a few minutes. Note down your resting heart rate. It is best to do this over several days and take an average.

Once you have determined these two heart rates, you can calculate your heart-rate reserve by subtracting the Hr min from the Hr max. You can then use this figure to determine training intensities (which is discussed at length in chapter nine).

THE HEART-RATE MONITOR AND MOUNTAIN BIKING Modern scientific training methods require athletes to exercise in prescribed training zones. These training zones are depicted not by speed but by how hard the heart is working. For example, if a mountain biker is riding uphill, the speed of the rider is reduced whereas their heart rate is increased. Conversely, going downhill their speed tends to increase while their heart rate decreases. If speed were the sole determinant of training then fitness effects would be determined by the terrain.

However, in mountain biking even the heart rate is subject to large fluctuations as a result of the course profile, riding surface and weather. This can present you with a potential problem if you are attempting to exercise in a prescribed training zone. With careful manipulation of gearing and cadence, it is possible when riding off road to maintain a heart rate that is within a few beats of the training zone. However, very specific heart-rate training should be performed on the road or on a turbo/resistance trainer.

HOW THE HEART-RATE MONITOR HELPS Specific intensities have a training effect on specific fitness components. It is therefore imperative that you work within a particular training zone, otherwise a different fitness component will be trained. Knowing your heart rate is important because exercise intensity can often be difficult to judge objectively. A lack of motivation or a stressful day at work can make exercise seem harder than it actually is.

Under these conditions it is easy to terminate a workout assuming that it has been of sufficient intensity to be of benefit, when in reality your cardiovascular system has not been taxed at all. In situations such as these, a heart-rate monitor is like having a personal trainer constantly reminding you to keep going. Conversely, working too hard can be counter productive and a heart-rate monitor can be a useful ally ensuring that you keep your easy days easy and that you are not getting carried away.

Later in this chapter we shall see how the morning heart rate and orthostatic heart rate can be used to determine whether you are fully recovered from a previous workout. The morning heart rate is also a good barometer of your well-being. If one morning your heart rate is abnormally high then this may indicate that you are about to become ill – training should therefore be delayed.

Resistance Trainer

A resistance trainer is a mechanical training device that allows you to ride indoors whilst remaining stationary. Most devices attach to the rear skewer and apply resistance to the rear wheel. How the resistance is applied varies. Some models use a fan (often referred to as a turbo trainer), others use magnets, or fluid. Nowadays, many health clubs and gymnasiums have stationary bicycle ergometers which allow for indoor training, and most of these have advanced functions such as power output, energy expenditure and heart-rate monitoring. Although these functions are of a distinct advantage, they are more than offset by the poor riding position and lack of clipless pedals. With these ergometers the riding position tends to be more upright than on a race-prepared mountain bike, whereas with resistance trainers you are riding on your own bike. Riding without clipless pedals will also interfere with maintaining the correct pedalling action (chapter twelve).

Resistance trainers make working within a prescribed heart-rate zone relatively easy and, despite being a rather monotonous way to train, they can be a valuable training tool. In addition to allowing an alternative medium for training when the weather is inclement, a resistance trainer enables you to perform accurate interval sessions without having to worry about undulating terrain or hazardous traffic situations.

As with the heart-rate monitors, the models and cost of resistance trainers differ quite considerably. The lower-priced models typically offer wind resistance which you alter by changing gear, and whilst providing adequate resistance, they can be noisy in use and often do not allow for a smooth pedal stroke. Fluid and magnetic resistance trainers are much quieter in use and most models allow the user to alter resistance by a remote lever which can be attached to the handlebars. Extra features on more expensive models include power output and cadence information. Some models are also computer compatible and enable you to simulate a race with other riders, or to ride your favourite international course. These extra features certainly go some way to alleviating the boredom traditionally associated with turbo trainer workouts.

Training Diary

An accurate training diary is an excellent source of training information. It allows you to view your training longitudinally and monitor your progress carefully over a period of time. Throughout your training year there will be times when you are required to perform fitness tests. These tests will give you a snapshot view of fitness status at that particular point in time. Fitness tests are naturally very intense and they place a lot of strain on your body. Because of this they must be used sparingly. Similarly, competing in a mountain bike race is the ultimate determinant of your fitness levels. However, racing is also physically demanding, and is limited mainly to the race season. There is therefore a large amount of time where your fitness is not checked. It is this gap that the training diary attempts to fill.

Completing a training diary on a daily basis can often be a laborious and monotonous task, but it takes less than five minutes to complete and is well worth the effort in the long run. In subsequent chapters I will detail how to design a training programme and how to fill in your training diary and ascribe workouts to specific days. In its most basic form a training diary allows you to check that you have done what you were supposed to have done. Over time you can analyse this and see if your workouts have had sufficient intensity. If there are any discrepancies then something is wrong and re-evaluation is needed. With a training diary, factors which may have otherwise gone unnoticed can easily come to light. Fluctuations in bodyweight or resting heart rate are important sources of information because they reflect your training status and well-being.

Nowadays, the majority of the computer-compatible heart-rate monitors come complete with logbook software, and update the daily entries each time a file is downloaded. The data can then be represented in graphical form and subsequently analysed. This is ideal if you are computer literate, but can be somewhat cumbersome if you are not.

WHAT TO INCLUDE The basic information you need for a training diary is as follows:
1. Morning heart-rate and orthostatic test
   The protocols for both of these tests are detailed at the end of this chapter. They are crucial sources of information when it comes to assessing your fitness status.

2. Desired and actual workout

The training programmes that are given in subsequent chapters will require you to exercise in precise heart-rate zones. However, this is often easier said than done. You should log both your prescribed workout and your actual workout.

3. Weather

Most of your training will be outdoors so it is at the mercy of the weather. Your mountain bike performance will fluctuate widely if your workouts are performed in headwinds, boggy mud, or extreme temperatures. As such you should record these conditions so that you can take them into account when you review your diary at a later date.

4. Sleep pattern

Your sleep pattern and recovery status are closely related. One or two poor nights' sleep can be accommodated without cause for concern. However, if there is a prolonged period where your sleep pattern is disturbed then this may reflect a hidden problem. Poor sleep is often associated with over-training.

5. Mental comments

Both your motivation and enthusiasm play crucial roles in your workouts, especially when the intensity is raised. Ultimately it is your brain that says when you've had enough and it is time to quit a workout. Record how you are feeling and how motivated you are.

6. Physical comments

Enter any physical feelings that you think are relevant. Are you feeling run down? Do your legs feel powerful? Are there any twinges? Write them all down.

A training diary is only of any real use if it is completed on a regular basis. At the end of every workout you should enter the information immediately while it is still fresh in your mind.

ANALYSIS OF THE TRAINING DIARY It is important that you analyse your training and evaluate your mountain bike performance on a regular basis. You should glance over your daily entries and compare your prescribed training with your actual workout. If there is any discrepancy between the two, try to deduce what the cause of the disparity is. On a weekly and monthly basis you should spend some time analysing your diary so far. See if you can find any relationships between your heart rates, your bodyweight, how you are feeling, what you ate, your sleep patterns and so on. Examine your good performances and also your bad ones. Is there a pattern emerging as to why you performed this way? It now becomes easy to see what factors improve your fitness. Obviously these should then be reproduced in the future, in order to maximise your fitness. Just as

Table 4: A Typical Page from a Mountain Biker's Training Diary

DATE: Monday		DATE: 17 April	
MORNING HR: 45	ORTHOSTATIC HR: 55	WEIGHT: 70 kg	
SLEEP DURATION 8 hours	WEATHER sunny – no wind		
DESIRED WORKOUT:	1 hour endurance ride @ ATI followed by 30 mins flexibility work.		
ACTUAL WORKOUT:	1 hour endurance ride, but some of it slightly below ATI threshold. Completed all 30 mins of flexibility work.		
HEART-RATE ZONE:	TIME IN: 50 mins	TIME ABOVE: 2 mins	TIME BELOW: 8 mins
PHYSICAL COMMENTS:	Felt pretty strong today, although legs were a little heavy from yesterday. Couldn't stay in training zone.		
MENTAL COMMENTS:	No problems here, I was raring to go!		
OTHER COMMENTS:	Ate a Powerbar 30 mins before the endurance ride and my energy levels were up for the whole ride.		

important, though, are the things that reduce your performance. Once you know what they are, you can avoid them.

THE WARM-UP

This is the procedure a rider performs prior to a competition or training in order to prepare, both physically and mentally, for the upcoming exercise. The aim of a warm-up is to reach an optimal body core and muscle temperature, which subsequently makes the body more efficient during exercise. The physical warming up of the muscles, tendons and ligaments makes them more elastic and less susceptible to strains and injury. Scientific studies have shown that far greater forces are required to tear a 'warmed-up' muscle compared to its cold counterpart. The increase in temperature also provides the optimal chemical environment within the muscles; increases the metabolic rate; and facilitates oxygen and fuel transportation to the working muscles. In other words, a warm-up primes your body's systems and gets them ready for exercise.

Many riders report feeling more 'psyched up' for a race after they have performed a warm-up. It gets them into the correct frame of mind prior to the race. It also improves their confidence because they feel that they can go 'all-out' without the fear of causing an injury.

Mountain Biking and the Warm-up

Start your warm-up with some general exercises for the whole body. Following a light jog, you should perform a routine of bodyweight exercises which move your muscles and joints through their full range of motion. Typical exercises include bodyweight squats, jogging on the spot, neck rolls and shoulder circles. Perform these until you break into a light sweat.

The emphasis of your warm-up should now focus on the specific muscles and joints that you will be using more intensely later on. Spin easy on your bike and slowly move up through the gears until you feel sufficiently warmed-up. It is important that you do not get fatigued during your warm-up and deplete your glycogen stores. Remember you are only *preparing* your body for exercise. You should now perform a series of stretches, paying particular emphasis to the muscles that you are going to be using. For information about stretching, see chapter five.

The benefits of a warm-up are transient and are only most effective for a couple of minutes afterwards. There is a gradual loss of the effects of a warm-up during inactivity and this is known as the warm-up decrement. This presents a problem for the mountain bike racer. Typically at a race it is advantageous to be at the front at the start in order to get the best racing line; however, as the best positions are taken early, there usually involves a waiting period of inactivity. A trade-off exists between the benefits of a good start position and those of a warm-up. In this situation it is best to leave it until the last possible moment before you line up. Wear some warm clothes and have someone collect them just prior to the start.

THE ROLE OF RECOVERY

Recovery is the name given to the physiological processes that occur in your body following training in order to restore it to its pre-exercise condition. The time your body takes to do this is called the recovery period. In order to optimise the effect of your mountain bike training, you must ensure that you are fully recovered between workouts and that you do not begin a subsequent training bout until you are fully recovered.

Clearly, the length of your recovery period can be a severe limiting factor to your training volume and ultimately your mountain bike fitness. For example, if rider A has a recovery period of 24 hours and rider B has a recovery period of 48 hours, rider A can perform a greater number of intense workouts in a given time period compared to rider B. It is therefore a distinct advantage to be able to facilitate your recovery period and there are a number of ways that you can achieve this.

Recovery following a training ride can actually be enhanced before and during the ride as well as after it. A thorough warm-up before training or competition reduces the trauma associated with exercise and so acts as a form of damage limitation with regard to post-exercise recovery. The replacement of spent carbohydrates during exercise is a potent factor in reducing the recovery period. Consume between half a litre and one litre of a 15 per cent carbohydrate drink every hour during your ride, as this aids the recovery of the energy production system (see chapter fifteen). Making sure that your body is fully hydrated throughout the exercise bout is of paramount importance, not only to performance, but also to ensuring full recovery.

It has been shown that during the recovery period muscle and phosphagen stores are replenished and the by-products of exercise – such as lactic acid and other metabolites – are removed. It is also during the recovery period that adaptation and protein replacement occur and you become fitter. As a result it is good practice to consume further carbohydrates following exercise so as to maximise glycogen storage.

There are two main physical procedures employed to enhance the recovery process, namely passive and active recovery. As the name suggests passive recovery involves doing nothing. Here the rider rests (typically lying down) with the assumption that recovery will be enhanced by reducing the energy demand of the body. This has only been shown to be effective for sub-maximal exercise, and as such is not really applicable to mountain bikers, despite it often being their first choice of recovery! Instead, active recovery has been found to be of greater benefit.

Active recovery, or cooling down or tapering off as it is otherwise known, involves light to moderate cycling following a vigorous ride. It is believed that active rest, in addition to aiding recovery, reduces the risk of injury and muscle soreness. For mountain bikers, active rest should involve cycling at an easy intensity for at least 30 minutes. Training status can greatly influence the rate of recovery. The fitter you are the shorter your recovery period will become. Taking a hot bath, shower or sauna after completion of a hard workout aids relaxation and recovery, as does ultrasound and massage. And of course good dietary practice is essential, for your body must have all the materials to hand if it is to rebuild itself.

Massage

In an ideal world you would receive a massage both before and after every bike ride from a qualified massage therapist. Lamentably, this tends to be the preserve only of the sponsored professional rider. Fortunately, however, it is possible to glean many of the benefits from self-massage. The benefits of massage for the mountain biker are many. Massaging a muscle, or group of muscles, helps to increase their temperature and improve the blood circulation to the area. This is ideal before a strenuous workout in order to prepare the muscle for the forthcoming exercise. It is also important after an intense ride because the improved circulation coupled with the mechanical action of massaging helps to remove metabolic by-products, such as lactic acid, from the muscles. Massaging also causes muscles to become more relaxed and is therefore a relevant precursor to stretching. It can also help to relieve painful muscle cramps – and of course it feels good!

SELF MASSAGE Self-massage is really very easy. All you have to do is rub and knead your muscles so that they relax. Relaxation of your muscles is the key. Don't press so hard that your muscles tense up as a result. The process is made a whole lot easier if you use massage oil or talc. If you have particularly hairy legs you may find the process painful because your hairs will get pulled as a result of the massaging action. If this is the case, you may want to consider shaving your legs, which is the reason why the professional mountain bikers do.

Below is a self-help massage guide to get you started. I've targeted the key muscles involved in mountain biking, though I'm sure there will be other muscles that will be aching after a hard day in the saddle. Don't be afraid to apply the principles to those ones as well – just remember not to massage any muscle that is injured.

Table 5: Self-massage Summary

MUSCLE	MASSAGE PROCEDURE
Soleus and gastrocnemius (calves)	These are a great muscles to massage. You should massage each calf with both hands, kneading deep into the muscle with your thumbs. You should start at the base of the calves and work up, as this helps remove any toxins.
Quadriceps (the large muscle on the front of the upper thigh)	After a tough mountain bike ride, the quadriceps are typically heavily fatigued and full of the by-products of exercise. You should massage the quadriceps with your fingers, thumbs and palms. Alternate deep kneading actions with lighter strokes. Again, you should work from the bottom upwards.

Hamstrings	The hamstring muscles are notoriously prone to
(the large muscle on the	cramping. A good post-ride massage will help prevent
back of the upper thigh)	this. Alternate deep kneading actions with lighter
	strokes. Again, you should work from the bottom
	upwards.
Glutes	Work the entire area with your fingers and thumbs.
(the muscles of your	Where it is particularly fleshy, knead deeply, but
backside)	avoid pressing too hard near bony areas (which could
	result in trapped nerves).

Recovery Tests

Having a good recovery period is often referred to as having 'good physiology' and is also an excellent indicator of your fitness and health status. Below are several tests that you can perform to assess the progress of your recovery ability. Remember to make sure that the conditions are similar each time you test.

RECOVERY RATE FIELD TEST 1

PURPOSE: This test monitors your ability to recover following an intense bout of exercise.

PROCEDURE: Find a quiet stretch of road with a long hill.

Ride as fast as possible up the hill (for no more than 2 minutes), keeping your pace as consistent as possible.

Record your time and your final heart rate (using a heart-rate monitor).

Rest for 3 minutes and then record your recovery heart rate.

Subtract your recovery heart rate from your exercise heart rate and note down the 'difference' figure.

Perform this test at regular intervals (about a month apart) and compare results. A greater 'difference' figure (or a faster time for the same figure) indicates an improved rate of recovery.

TESTING TIP: Use the same location, same start and finish points, comparable weather, and ensure that you are fully recovered beforehand.

RECOVERY RATE FIELD TEST 2

PURPOSE: This test monitors your ability to recover in between a series of repeated exercise bouts.

PROCEDURE: On a flat section of open ground, place two markers 60 m apart.

Approach the first marker and sprint maximally to the next one. Have an assistant record your time.

Recover for 20 seconds by cycling at an easy pace.

Repeat the above procedure until you have completed eight sprints.

You can now convert your times into a fatigue index which can be used to assess your ability to recover between sprints. In theory, if all your sprints are the same then you have fully recovered during each rest period. If you fail to recover fully then you should notice an increase in sprint time as the test progresses. Use the following equation to calculate your fatigue index:

$$\frac{(T7 + T8)}{2} - \frac{(T1 + T2)}{2} = D$$

$$\text{Fatigue Index (\%)} = \frac{D}{(T1 + T2)/2} \times 100$$

A low Fatigue Index score indicates a good ability to recover.

0% = Full recovery

100% = Fully fatigued

TESTING TIP: In order to get meaningful and accurate results, don't pace yourself during this test; go maximally on every sprint.

ORTHOSTATIC HEART-RATE TEST

PURPOSE: The orthostatic (standing) test is a simple procedure for monitoring recovery status. It is based on changes in heart-rate values caused by standing erect following a period of being supine (lying down face-up).

PROCEDURE: Lie supine and rest for 15 minutes.

Record your heart rate.

Stand up and, after 15 seconds, record your heart rate again.

Subtract the supine heart-rate value from the standing heart-rate value.

The typical figure for this value for a fully recovered individual is below 15 beats per minute. If it is greater than 20 then you have not fully recovered from your training.

TESTING TIP: This information is only relevant if you do it every day, so get into the habit of performing this test every morning.

MORNING HEART-RATE TEST

Every morning, shortly after waking, take a heart-rate reading. Over a period of time you should be able to establish a typical waking heart rate. As you become fitter this value should drop. However, a rise in morning heart rate usually signifies incomplete recovery.

SUBJECTIVE RECOVERY TEST

After you have been following a training schedule for an extended period of time you will gain experience from the heart-rate monitor and associated feelings and be able to 'read', as well as monitor, your body. Typical feelings of complete recovery include a strong desire to train, good sleeping pattern, positive attitude, and a feeling of well-being and good health.

5. FLEXIBILITY

BENEFITS OF FLEXIBILITY

Flexibility is perhaps the most underestimated and undervalued component of mountain bike fitness. You may be forgiven for thinking that its role in mountain biking is limited, especially if you compare it to other sports such as gymnastics where the need for flexibility is more obvious. However, scratch beneath the surface and it soon becomes apparent that flexibility plays a major part in your mountain biking fitness, and it can have a major influence on the longevity of your racing career.

When implemented correctly, a stretching programme can offer many benefits to the mountain biker which include:

ENHANCED PHYSICAL FITNESS As we have already discussed in chapter one, flexibility is an integral component of your physical fitness. If flexibility is your weak link, an improvement in this area will complete your fitness jigsaw and make you a more rounded athlete.

IMPROVEMENT IN POSTURE Poor posture can often be traced to muscular imbalance and inferior flexibility. This is especially rife in sports such as mountain biking where the posture of the rider is hunched up and the limbs are rarely stretched. An improvement in your flexibility will enable your posture to return to normal and give you the added benefit of avoiding the auxiliary problems associated with chronic joint misalignment.

REDUCED MUSCLE TENSION AND IMPROVED PERFORMANCE Tight, inflexible muscles will lead to tension that will be both uncomfortable and unhealthy. An improvement in your flexibility will result in unrestricted muscles and less tension. This will also improve your mountain bike efficiency, because your working muscles will have to overcome less resistance and therefore use less energy.

REDUCED MUSCLE SORENESS Research indicates that if a stretching programme is performed after rigorous exercise it will help facilitate recovery and alleviate delayed muscle soreness. This will mean that you can train sooner and, as a result, you will get fitter quicker.

REDUCED RISK OF INJURY TO JOINTS, MUSCLES, TENDONS AND LIGAMENTS Flexibility training will increase the range of motion at your joints. If your joints are suddenly moved in an unfamiliar action, such as during a crash, then the likelihood of walking away without an injury will be greater if you are flexible.

PREPARATION OF THE MUSCLES FOR THE IMPENDING EXERCISE Because of the responses highlighted above, performing stretching exercises prior to exercising will help increase the readiness of your muscles and improve their response to exercise. In a race scenario this means you will be ready from the very start – not after a few minutes once they have been loosened.

INCREASED MENTAL AND PHYSICAL RELAXATION The act of stretching not only physically slackens your muscles, but, if performed correctly, can also lead to a state of mental relaxation.

ENHANCED DEVELOPMENT OF BODY AWARENESS Feeling the stretching and tension in your muscles leads to an improved neuro-muscular knowledge which in turn increases your kinaesthetic awareness.

A REDUCTION IN THE TENDENCY OF MUSCLES TO SHORTEN AND TIGHTEN FOLLOWING TRAINING When you are mountain biking, there is very little time during the pedalling action when your legs are straight. They are denied the opportunity fully to extend or flex, and because of this the range of motion at the knee is limited. As a result the muscles on the back of your thigh (the hamstrings) are never stretched. This condition can lead to a gradual shortening of the muscle and consequent injury unless an appropriate stretching programme is implemented.

ENJOYMENT Performing stretching exercises feels good.

Flexibility, like any other component of physical fitness, is subject to the principles of training, and if performed correctly it can drastically increase your performance. However, if performed erroneously, stretching may hinder your mountain bike progress. The most common mistakes include:

INAPPROPRIATE WARM-UP Muscles, joints and connective tissue are more susceptible to injuries and tears if they are cold. Subjecting your body to a flexibility workout is asking for trouble if you haven't adequately warmed up. It follows, therefore, that it is counterproductive to use stretching solely as your warm-up. In order to reduce the likelihood of muscle, tendon and ligament impairment, you should only include your stretching regimen after your general warm-up, when your muscles are warmer and more pliable.

INADEQUATE REST BETWEEN WORKOUTS In order for your muscles and connective tissue to adapt to the stretches and fully supercompensate, you are going to have to give them time. If you are a beginner, or are new to flexibility training, you should avoid performing rigorous stretching protocols on consecutive days.

OVER-STRETCHING We all have the potential to improve significantly our flexibility; but only if we are patient. Like all aspects of our fitness, the whole process takes time and cannot be rushed. Many beginners want immediate gratification and will endeavour to reach further, even if it hurts. Over-stretching your muscles and connective tissue is obviously dangerous and will inevitably lead to injury.

PERFORMING THE STRETCHES INCORRECTLY Incorrect technique when stretching can often be worse than performing no flexibility work at all. Because you are placing your muscles, joints and connective tissue under considerable strain, it is imperative that you use only safe exercises and adhere to strict form.

STRETCHING METHODS

There are several types of stretching methods available for you to use, the predominant ones being: static; ballistic; and proprioceptive neuro-muscular facilitation (PNF). Ballistic stretching involves dynamic 'bouncing' in order to increase the range of motion at a joint. If it is practised by an unsupervised novice it can rapidly lead to injury. PNF stretching is a more complicated form of stretching and can also be dangerous if performed by the unskilled. We will focus solely on static stretching, as this method is effective, relatively safe, can be done on your own with minimal equipment, and is applicable to mountain biking.

Before we go any further it is important that you have an understanding of the physiology of a muscle and what happens to it when it is stretched. Deep within a skeletal muscle there are special receptors known as muscle spindles. These are safety mechanisms that are sensitive to stretch. If a muscle is elongated rapidly, or over-stretched, the muscle spindle counteracts this potentially harmful action by initiating a reflex message via the spinal cord which causes the muscle to contract. This is known as a stretch reflex and is a preventative measure to stop the muscle from tearing. This stretch reflex lasts for about ten seconds, and then if no harm has been done it switches off. With the stretch reflex turned off, it is now possible to stretch a little further until the stretch reflex is initiated once again. To profit from this and reap the maximum effect, you should hold your stretches for at least 30 seconds.

In accordance with the specificity principle, each flexibility exercise you perform should only stretch the muscles that you are attempting to stretch. Isolating the individual muscles means that you only have to overcome the resistance of the antagonist (opposing) muscle alone. This offers a more sensitive gauge of the intensity of the stretch and ultimately gives you more control over the exercise thus minimising the risk of injury.

The potential risk of injury from performing a particular stretch must be taken into consideration from a personal perspective. A mild amount of discomfort is often associated with stretching, but if you experience any pain before, during, or after stretching you must stop immediately and identify the cause (which will probably be one of the four common mistakes mentioned earlier). Although a particular stretch may be highly regarded as being effective in enhancing flexibility, you must always be aware that it may not complement your biomechanics or injury history. If this is the case then omit the troublesome exercise from your programme and substitute it with another more appropriate one. There are many excellent books on the market dedicated to sports injuries, rehabilitation and stretching, containing a plethora of exercises for you to choose from.

The following stretching programme is designed to increase your flexibility and complement your mountain biking. After having performed the exercises you should not feel sore. If you do then you have over-stretched and caused microscopic trauma to the muscle. To avoid over-stretching, you should perform the exercise until you are able to feel the tension in the muscle, but no more. Exhale as you move into the stretch, hold the position for 30 seconds breathing rhythmically, then move out of the stretch with as much care as you went in to it. You should aim to perform as many sets of the stretch as it takes in order to reach your maximum range of motion (usually four). Perform the stretches in the order they are given. It is important to note that if you are stretching prior to a ride, rather than to increase flexibility per se, you should not work the muscles to the point of fatigue. Save your energy for your riding.

STRETCHING PROGRAMME

NECK ROLLS

PURPOSE: During mountain biking the jarring effect of the trail combined with the bracing of the shoulder muscles can lead to tension in the neck area. The following stretch targets the entire neck and relieves muscular tension.

PROCEDURE: In a standing position, gently and slowly roll your neck through its full range of motion. Do this ten times in each direction.

STRETCHING TIP: As you roll your neck through its full range of motion, there will be tight spots where the neck muscles will feel taut. When you encounter one of these, stop and hold the stretch for several seconds before continuing.

Neck rolls

NECK SIDE STRETCH

PURPOSE: This is an excellent stretch for releasing neck and shoulder tension.

PROCEDURE: Stand upright, looking straight ahead with your hands clasped behind your back.

Now lower your right ear to your right shoulder, whilst simultaneously pulling your left arm downwards with your right hand.

STRETCHING TIP: Hold the stretch, relax and then repeat with the other side.

Neck side stretch

ARM AND SHOULDER STRETCH

PURPOSE: This stretch promotes mobility in the shoulder area.

PROCEDURE: Stand upright with your hands clasped behind your lower back.

Keeping your arms straight, lift your arms behind you in a backwards arch. You should feel the stretch in your shoulders, across your chest and in your arms.

Hold the stretch and relax.

STRETCHING TIP: To maximise this stretch, push your chest out and keep your chin tucked in.

Arm and shoulder stretch

OVERHEAD ARM AND SHOULDER STRETCH

PURPOSE: This exercise also increases shoulder mobility, but also stretches the back of the upper arm (the triceps).

PROCEDURE: Stand upright and lift your left arm straight up.

Bend your left elbow, and with your right hand gently pull your left elbow behind your head.

Hold the stretch and relax, then repeat with the other arm.

STRETCHING TIP: You may find that you have one shoulder that is more flexible than the other. If this is so spend a little more time on your weak shoulder and bring it up to par.

Overhead arm
and shoulder

FOREARM STRETCH

PURPOSE: Trail buzz and downhill biking fatigue the forearm muscles very quickly. This exercise is a great way to improve the flexibility of your forearm muscles and facilitate their recovery.

PROCEDURE: Kneel down on your hands and knees. Rotate your hands outwards so that your thumbs are on the outside and your fingers are pointing back towards your knees.

Keeping your arms straight and your palms flat on the floor, slowly lean back until you can feel a comfortable stretch in your forearm muscles.

Forearm stretch

Hold the stretch and relax.

STRETCHING TIPS: Make sure you keep the heel of your hand on the floor at all times.

Most mountain bikers have relatively tight forearms, so start off gradually and don't force the stretch.

SIDE STRETCH

PURPOSE: This exercise targets the muscles on the side of your torso (the obliques) and is a great stretch to do after a long day in the saddle.

PROCEDURE: Stand upright with your feet about shoulder-width apart.

Raise your left hand over your head and place your right hand on the outside of your right thigh.

Slowly and carefully bend to your right. Let your right hand slide down your right thigh. You can use your right hand for support if you need it. You should feel a comfortable stretch along the left side of your torso.

Hold the stretch and carefully and deliberately return to the start position.

Repeat with the other side.

STRETCHING TIPS: Make sure that you only bend to the side. Do not lean forwards or backwards.

Avoid the temptation to hold your breath when you are performing this stretch. Make a conscious effort to breathe normally.

In the beginning, only hold the stretch for ten seconds. As you become more comfortable with the exercise, gradually increase the time that you spend in the stretch until you can do it for 30 seconds.

Side stretch

KNEELING LOWER BACK STRETCH

PURPOSE: This is an excellent exercise to increase the range of motion in your vertebrae and to loosen any knotted or tight muscles in your back.

PROCEDURE: Kneel down on your hands and knees. Then, without moving your arms or legs, simultaneously lower your head whilst arching your back upwards. Hold the stretch and relax.

Then perform the reverse of the above. Raise your head whilst lowering your spine to form a hollow. Hold the stretch and relax.

STRETCHING TIPS: Make the movements slow and deliberate.

Kneeling lower back stretch

Avoid the temptation to hold your breath when you are performing this stretch. Make a conscious effort to breathe normally.

ABDOMINALS/LOWER BACK STRETCH

PURPOSE: This stretching exercise increases the range of motion in your vertebrae and also stretches your abdominal muscles. It is an excellent stretch to perform after you have done a set of sit-ups.

PROCEDURE: Lie on your front, as if you are about to perform a press-up. Then, without moving your hands or feet, straighten your arms and arch your back.

Look upwards, so that your whole spine hyper-extends and you can feel a comfortable stretch in your abdominals.

Hold the stretch and relax.

STRETCHING TIP: Avoid the temptation to hold your breath when you are performing this stretch. Make a conscious effort to breathe normally.

Abdominals/lower back stretch

SEATED TWIST STRETCH

PURPOSE: This exercise targets your upper and lower back, as well as your hip area. It is an excellent stretch to perform after a long day in the saddle.

PROCEDURE: Sit down with both legs extended in front of you. Then bend your left leg and cross it over your right, so that the heel of your left foot is touching the outside of your right knee.

With your left hand resting behind you for support, rotate your torso towards your bent knee and place your right elbow on the outside of your left knee.

Seated twist stretch

Turn your head over your left shoulder and look behind you. At the same time apply controlled pressure to your left knee with your right elbow.

Hold the stretch and relax, then repeat with the other side.

STRETCHING TIPS: Throughout the stretch, ensure that your hips do not move.

Avoid the temptation to hold your breath when you are performing this stretch. Make a conscious effort to breathe normally.

GROIN STRETCH

PURPOSE: This is a good exercise to improve the flexibility in your hip and groin area.

PROCEDURE: Sit down with the soles of your feet together, then bring them as close to

your groin as possible. Hold your ankles and bend forward slightly at the hips whilst maintaining a straight back. Hold this stretch for a few seconds.

Now gently press down on your knees with your elbows until you feel a good stretch in your groin.

Groin stretch

Hold the stretch and relax.

STRETCHING TIPS: Only bend slightly forward at the hips. Do not round your back.

Only after you have settled into the first part of the stretch, and you are stable, should you proceed with stretching the groin area.

STANDING CALF STRETCH

PURPOSE: During a mountain bike ride your calves are continually worked. They are involved in every pedal stroke and have to support your bodyweight when you stand up on your pedals and coast. Flexible calf muscles will result in a more ergonomic pedal stroke and reduce the likelihood of the muscles cramping.

PROCEDURE: Stand in front of a wall and step forward with your left foot. Assume a position as if you were attempting to push the wall over and make sure that both of your feet are pointing straight ahead.

Keeping your feet parallel and your heels on the ground, slowly bend your left knee and move your hips forward. Throughout the stretch, you should keep your right leg straight

Standing calf stretch

and your lower back flat. You should feel a stretch in your right calf muscle.

Hold the stretch and relax, then repeat with the other leg.

STRETCHING TIP: Keep your heels on the floor throughout the stretch.

HAMSTRING STRETCH

PURPOSE: Mountain bikers notoriously have tight hamstrings. This is because the hamstring muscle is rarely stretched during the cycling action. Once you are off the bike, tight hamstrings can exert an uneven pull on your pelvis and cause postural problems. They are often the cause of lower back pain.

PROCEDURE: Sit down with both legs extended in front of you and place the sole of your right foot against the inside of your left thigh.

Without bending your left leg, lean forward at the hips and try to hold your left ankle.

Hold the stretch and relax, then repeat with the other side.

Hamstring stretch

STRETCHING TIPS: Do not dip your head during the stretch. Look at the foot of your outstretched leg.

Keep the foot of your outstretched leg pointing straight upwards.

Ensure that the quadriceps muscles of your outstretched leg are relaxed.

QUADRICEPS STRETCH

PURPOSE: This is a good exercise for stretching the large muscle group on the front of your thigh (the quadriceps). It is a particularly good exercise for bringing a bit of life back into tired legs.

PROCEDURE: Stand upright on your right leg and bring your left heel to your buttock. Take hold of your left foot with your left hand.

With your left knee pointing towards the floor, gently pull your left foot backwards until you feel a stretch in your frontal thigh.

Hold the stretch and relax, then repeat with the other leg.

STRETCHING TIPS: If you have problems balancing whilst holding this stretch, hold on to something for support, although with practice you should be able to do it free-standing.

Quadriceps stretch

This stretch can also be performed on the floor. Lying face down, reach behind you with your left hand and hold onto your left foot. Then continue with the above procedure.

As we have discussed in chapter four, stretching should not only be a workout in its own right, but it should also be part of the cooling down process because it helps to reduce muscle fatigue and soreness. Furthermore, if you are still sore or tight the day after an intense ride, perform a light stretching routine to help reduce the lingering tenderness and tautness.

Stretching on the Bike

There are times whilst you are on your mountain bike when it may be advantageous to perform some stretches. If you are involved in an ultra-endurance event, or a touring expedition, you can relieve your tired muscles and inject a bit of life back into them with a few simple stretches. If you are in a race you may need to stretch a muscle to prevent it from cramping. The following simple stretches can be performed when you are on the move. It stands to reason that these exercises should only be performed on easy terrain, where you can see well ahead, and where you are not going to cause any harm either to yourself or to another rider.

BACK/NECK STRETCH

PURPOSE: This stretch can be used to alleviate tense shoulder and back muscles. You can also use it to help relieve tired muscles in your neck that have become fatigued as a result of maintaining an upright head position so that you can look forwards and keep an eye on the terrain.

PROCEDURE: At a safe section of terrain, sit down and coast.

Arch your back and allow your chin touch to your chest. Stretch this position as far as possible.

Back/neck stretch

Hold this stretch momentarily, then resume your normal riding position.

STRETCHING TIP: If the terrain permits, repeat the above procedure as many times as is necessary.

QUADRICEPS STRETCH

PURPOSE: This is an excellent way of refreshing your quadriceps muscles during a hard ride or race. In order to perform this stretch you need a good sense of balance and co-ordination. It is therefore wise to practise this stretch on your training rides rather than for the first time in a race.

PROCEDURE: At a safe section of terrain, sit down and coast.

Shift your bodyweight over your saddle and unclip your fatigued leg. Bring your right foot up to your buttocks and hold onto it with your right hand.

Quadriceps stretch

Hold the stretch for as long as possible, then return your foot to the pedal.

STRETCHING TIP: If terrain permits, repeat with the other leg if necessary.

LOWER BACK STRETCH

PURPOSE: It is very common in mountain bike racing for the lower back to be a source of pain and great discomfort. If you find yourself suffering from lower back fatigue, the following stretch will give you a bit of respite from it.

PROCEDURE: At a safe section of terrain, coast. Then shift your body forwards and downwards as if you are about to sit on the top tube just behind your stem.

Hover above the top tube without actually sitting on it.

Simultaneously stick your chest out and form a hollow in your lower back.

Return to your normal riding position.

STRETCHING TIP: Repeat this procedure as many times as is necessary.

Lower back stretch

CALF STRETCH

PURPOSE: After prolonged sections of terrain where you have had to remain out of the saddle – such as a particularly fearsome downhill section – your calves may

become fatigued and feel as if they are on fire. To relieve this sensation and to avoid cramp try the following stretch.

PROCEDURE: At a safe section of terrain, coast. Then stand out of the saddle with the cranks horizontal.

With only a slight bend in your legs, slowly lower your heels so that they are below the pedal axles. You should feel the stretch in your calf muscles.

Calf stretch

STRETCHING TIP: The stretch should be most intense in the rear leg, so repeat the procedure having first altered the cranks 180°.

6. STRENGTH TRAINING

THE THEORY OF STRENGTH TRAINING

Strength training is a very important, yet often overlooked, aspect of mountain bike fitness training. The very nature of mountain biking places a great demand on the muscles of the body, especially those in the limbs and lower back as they are forced to absorb the shock of the undulating terrain, the drop-offs and the inevitable crashes. There may also be times in your racing career when you are forced to carry your bike for various sections of the course. Lifting a lightweight mountain bike may not sound too bad right now, but when you're on your last lap and your bike is caked in mud it will feel like an old 30-pound clunker. It is therefore advantageous for you to develop a sound muscular infrastructure so that you can accommodate the physical beatings that mountain bike racing throws at you. Weak auxiliary muscles also play a critical role in the loss of form when a rider is fatigued. This is evident at races across all the disciplines of mountain biking. Cross-country riders completing their final lap, or downhill competitors on the last stretch of the course, often display poor form because their muscles are fatigued and won't respond. This inevitably leads to a subsequent drop in riding efficiency, which could have been avoided if strengthening exercises had been included in their training programme.

You should incorporate strength training into your programme, not to develop muscle hypertrophy per se, but for the rather less cosmetic role of facilitating muscular power and strength. In addition to these prized components, strengthening exercises also improve all-round body conditioning by bringing under-developed muscles up to par. Unfortunately, mountain biking on its own promotes muscular imbalance. Certain muscles, such as the quadriceps (the large muscles on the front of your thigh), are continually used and as a result they adapt by becoming bigger and stronger. Other muscles, such as the hamstrings (the muscles on the back of your thigh), are stressed less and so do not develop at the same rate. If left unchecked, this can create an uneven pull on the knee joint and can eventually lead to a chronic injury. It is therefore important to perform strengthening exercises for the hamstrings in order to avoid potential knee problems. Similarly, mountain biking stresses the lower back muscles more than it stresses the abdominal muscles. This predicament causes an uneven pull on the spine and can lead to postural deficiencies. Again it is important to perform strengthening exercises for the weaker muscles in order to restore correct muscle balance.

As good as it is, strength work should only supplement your training and not detract from it. By its very nature, strength training is an intense activity and it can cause you serious damage if you are lifting weights with poor technique. It is therefore imperative that you maintain the correct lifting procedure at all times. An injured body means time out of the saddle, which in turn means a subsequent reduction in your mountain bike fitness due to a detraining effect. The key here is to leave your ego behind when you visit the gym and lift conservatively. Remember you are a mountain biker, not a body builder.

You should perform two strength workouts per week, with each one lasting no longer than 60 minutes. As with all of your training, you should divide your strength work up into distinct phases (see chapter eight) with each phase focusing on a particular aspect of your strength. Your first strength phase is a general conditioning programme which should run in conjunction with your foundation phase and last for between 10 to 15 weeks. During this phase you should concentrate on developing all-round, well-balanced strength. Your aim during this period should be to develop a flawless strength base upon which you can build during the following phases.

The second stage is a power and strength programme which should supplement your preparation phases (P1 and P2 phases; see chapter eight) and should last for approximately 15 weeks. It is during this period that you will be lifting your heaviest weights. The third and final phase is muscular endurance based and should coincide with your race season.

STRENGTH TRAINING TIPS

No matter what training phase you are in, there are several guidelines to which you should constantly adhere:

1. Prior to every strength training session you should perform a thorough warm-up. If you are scheduled to lift heavy weights, as in the power and strength programme, it is advisable to increase the length of the warm-up accordingly. Following the warm-up you should then perform a full body-stretching routine, paying particular attention to the muscles that you are going to exercise.

2. Perform all of the strength exercises in a slow, controlled manner. Ensure that you always concentrate on strict form and do not let your execution of the

exercise become sloppy in order to lift heavy weights. Concentrate and focus on the muscle, or muscles, you are exercising.

3. It is advisable to perform strength work with a training partner. Training partners are an invaluable help, not only with maintaining your motivation, but also with ensuring that you are adhering to strict form.

4. In each phase there is a recommended repetition range with a minimum and a maximum number. When starting the phase you should select a weight that allows you to perform the minimum number of repetitions and no more, no matter how hard you try. As you become stronger your repetitions will increase. Once you reach the maximum number of repetitions, increase the weight so that you can only perform the minimum number of repetitions. And so on.

5. When working with machines, ensure they are set up for your biomechanics. Most strength-training machines are fully adjustable. I know it can be time consuming to adjust the machines every time you use them, but it is a necessary evil when it comes to avoiding injury. Trying to fit into a machine that has been adjusted to suit someone else will place undesired forces on your joints, muscles and connective tissue and will result in an injury. Wherever possible, try to align your joints with the appropriate pivot on the machines.

6. Do not perform strength training on consecutive days; allow time for your muscles to recover and rebuild between workouts. If you are pushed for time, it is possible to perform strength workouts on two consecutive days, but only if you split your workouts into upper and lower body exercises. If you work your upper body one day, and then your lower body the next, no two body parts are stressed on both days.

7. Don't forget to breathe when you are exercising. Holding your breath whilst performing the exercises will only lead to dizziness. As a rule of thumb, breathe out on exertion and breathe in when relaxing. If this method does not suit you, just breathe normally as that is infinitely better for you than not breathing.

8. Youth category riders should only perform strength exercises using their body weight and should not perform weight training exercises.

9. Current research indicates that strength training causes muscles to shorten. In order to offset this potential problem, after your workout you should make sure that you perform the appropriate stretches for the muscles that you have been working.

STRENGTH TRAINING PROGRAMME

General Conditioning Phase
This is the first of your strength training phases and will last between 10 and 15

weeks. If you are new to weight lifting, or it has been some time since you last visited a gym, then it is wise to get some expert tuition for your first few visits to the weights room. Included here is a list of exercises that you should perform as part of this strength phase. If you are a veteran of the weights room and you already know your maximum strength for each of the exercises, the amount of weight that you will lift in this phase will be between 50 and 65 per cent of your maximum. You should perform between 15 and 20 repetitions of each exercise. If, however, you don't know your maximum strength in each exercise, I urge you not to try to find out. Lifting very heavy weights is an unnecessary injury risk; instead, you should use the first few visits to the gym to ascertain the correct weight so that you can perform the desired number of repetitions and no more. You should also use these first few workouts to concentrate on the correct lifting technique.

The strengthening exercises for this programme are designed in a circuit, with no body part worked on consecutive stations. This allows the fatigued muscles time to recover while the other muscles are working. You should perform one set on a particular exercise and then move straight on to the next exercise with little rest in between. It is designed like this in order to make efficient use of your time in the gym. It is not intended to give you any aerobic benefit. Your aerobic fitness level should easily be able to cope with the schedule without becoming unduly stressed.

You do not have to go to a specialist gym in order to strength train for mountain biking. It is possible to perform a wide range of strength exercises at home with the minimum of equipment. The basic equipment you need for an adequate home gym includes barbell, dumb-bells, bench, squat racks and chin-up bar. Even if you do train at a commercial gym, not all of the exercises, or the machines listed in this chapter, are going to be available to you. Where this is the case, replace the impractical exercises with similar ones that work the same muscles. There are many excellent books on the market, dedicated solely to weight training, that contain numerous strength exercises for you to choose from.

The Exercises
LEG EXTENSION
PURPOSE: This is an excellent exercise for isolating and developing the large muscle group on the front of the thigh (the quadriceps). This exercise also helps to prepare the quadriceps for the subsequent leg exercises.

PROCEDURE: Sit on the leg extension machine and place your feet under the padded rollers. Adjust the machine so that the axis of your knee is in line with the pivot on the machine.

Slowly extend your legs until they are straight, then pause momentarily in this position. You should be able to feel your quadriceps working.

Slowly lower the weight back to the starting position and repeat for the required number of repetitions.

EXERCISE TIPS: Keep your movements slow and deliberate.

Keep tension in your quadriceps throughout the entire range of the exercise by not putting the weight down. Initiate the upward phase of the movement before the cable goes slack. Do not allow the weights to bang together.

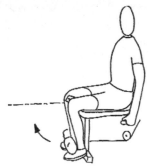

Leg extension

LEG CURL

PURPOSE: The exercise is the opposite of the one above. It strengthens and develops the large muscle group on the back of the thighs (the hamstrings) and when performed in conjunction with the leg extension it ensures proper muscle balance at the knee. This exercise also helps prepare the hamstrings for the subsequent leg exercises.

PROCEDURE: Lie face-down on the leg curl machine, and place your heels under the pads. Adjust your position so that the axis of your knee is in line with the pivot on the machine.

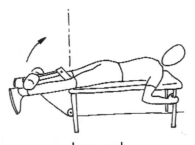

Leg curl

Slowly flex your legs and bring your heels as close to your buttocks as possible. Pause momentarily in this fully flexed position. You should be able to feel your hamstrings contracting.

Slowly lower the weight back to the starting position and repeat for the required number of repetitions.

EXERCISE TIPS: Move only at the knees. Do not select a weight that forces you to use your upper body and arch your back.

As with the leg extensions, keep tension in your muscles throughout the entire range of the exercise by not putting the weight down. Initiate the upward phase of the movement before the cable goes slack. Do not allow the weights to bang together.

LAT PULL-DOWNS

PURPOSE: Mountain biking requires a great deal of upper body strength. This exercise targets the large muscles on the upper back (the latissimus dorsi), the

Lat pull-downs

rear of shoulders (the posterior deltoids) and the front of the upper arm (the biceps). It also helps improve your grip strength.

PROCEDURE: Take hold of the pull-down bar, with a slightly wider than shoulder-width overhand grip. Sit down on the machine and put your knees under the retainer pads.

Lean back slightly. Maintaining a slightly arched back, slowly and smoothly pull the bar down until it touches the top of your chest. Hold this position momentarily.

Slowly and smoothly return the bar to arm's length and feel the stretch in your muscles. Repeat for the desired number of repetitions.

EXERCISE TIPS: This exercise is most effective if you minimise any movement from the waist; the only body parts that should be moving are your arms.

For maximum effect, stretch the muscles at the top of every repetition.

SQUAT

PURPOSE: This is an ideal exercise for developing immense leg strength. It targets the muscles in the entire lower body, but it is the quadriceps that are affected the most.

Squat

PROCEDURE: Stand upright with your feet shoulder-width apart, a barbell resting across the back of your shoulders.

Keeping your head up and your back straight, slowly bend your knees until they are parallel to the floor.

Slowly push upwards, back to the starting position, and repeat for the required number of repetitions.

EXERCISE TIPS: Extra special care should be taken when performing squats due to the amount of strain placed on the vertebrae. Make sure you maintain a straight back at all times.

Throughout the exercise, make sure that your knees stay over, and in line with, your feet at all times.

Do not allow your knees to splay outwards, or let them go below 90°.

It is a good idea to perform this exercise in front of a full-length mirror so that you can keep an eye on your technique at all times.

This exercise can be made more comfortable if you place a low block of wood under your heels.

SEATED ROWS

PURPOSE: This is another great exercise for targeting the large muscles of the upper back (the latissimus dorsi). It also develops the rear of the shoulders (the posterior deltoids) and the front of the upper arm (biceps) and it also helps improve your grip strength.

PROCEDURE: Sit down on the seated row machine. Place your feet on the foot plates, and have a slight bend in your knees.

Seated rows

Take hold of the handle and slowly pull it towards your abdominals. At the same time arch your back. Throughout the exercise, do not lean too far forwards or backwards.

Slowly return to the starting position, lowering the weight until you feel a stretch in your latissimus muscles. Repeat for the required number of repetitions.

EXERCISE TIPS: You can make this exercise more mountain bike specific by using a grip width which is similar to that on your mountain bike.

With some machines it is possible to change the type of bar that you can use. If this is the case at your gym, alternate with a bar that allows a vertical grip similar to that of pulling back on bar ends.

LEG PRESS

PURPOSE: This exercise develops the same muscles as the squat, but because of its range of motion, the action is similar to pushing down on a pedal.

PROCEDURE: Sit in the leg press machine, and place your feet shoulder-width apart on the foot plate.

Remove the safety bars, bend your knees and slowly lower the weight.

When your knees are bent at right angles, slowly press the weight back to the starting position. Repeat for the required number of repetitions.

EXERCISE TIPS: Keep the tension in your legs throughout the full range of movement by not locking your knees out.

Leg press

Vary your foot position in each workout. Shoulder-width apart develops all-round leg strength. A closer foot position targets the outer thigh, while a slightly wider foot position develops the inner thigh.

BENCH PRESS

PURPOSE: The bench press develops the large muscles on the chest (pectoral muscles), the muscles on the front of the shoulders (the anterior deltoids) and the back of the upper arm (the triceps).

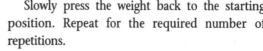

PROCEDURE: Lie face up on a bench that is equipped with racks. Take hold of the barbell a little wider than shoulder-width apart. Press the barbell off the rack.

Slowly lower the weight until it touches your lower pectoral muscles. Ensure that throughout the execution of this exercise your elbows are pointing outwards.

Slowly press the weight back to the starting position. Repeat for the required number of repetitions.

Bench press

EXERCISE TIPS: Keep your elbows out to the sides throughout the movement and keep your wrists directly above your elbows.

Do not arch your back.

Do not bounce the weight on your chest in order to get extra momentum.

CALF RAISE

PURPOSE: This exercise isolates the calf muscles (gastrocnemius) and is an excellent way to develop their dynamic strength.

PROCEDURE: Stand on your toes on the blocks of the calf raise machine. Place your shoulders under the pads.

Keeping your back straight, and your knees slightly bent, slowly raise up onto the balls of your feet. Hold this position momentarily and feel the contraction in your calves.

Slowly lower your heels as far as possible and hold this position momentarily. You should feel a stretching sensation within the calves.

Slowly press the weight back to the starting position and repeat for the required number of repetitions.

Calf raise

EXERCISE TIPS: Only use your calf muscles to lift the weight. Do not use body movements to help generate momentum.

Ensure that your range of motion is from full stretch at the bottom to fully contracted at the top.

Keep your back straight and your knees slightly bent.

SIDE LATERALS

PURPOSE: This exercise develops the middle of the shoulder muscles (medial deltoids), and contributes greatly to your upper body strength.

PROCEDURE: Stand upright with your arms down at your sides, and a dumb-bell in each hand.

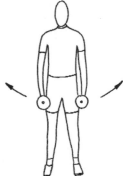

With a slight bend in your elbows, slowly raise your arms out to your sides in a big arc. Lift the weights to a point slightly higher than your shoulders.

Slowly lower the weights to the starting position and repeat for the required number of repetitions.

EXERCISE TIP: Ensure that you are lifting the dumb-bells straight out to the sides and not too far forwards or backwards.

Side laterals

BICEPS CURL

PURPOSE: The biceps curl works the muscle on the front of your upper arm (the biceps) and helps develop your grip strength.

PROCEDURE: Stand upright with your feet about shoulder-width apart. Take hold of a barbell with an underhand grip. Your grip should also be shoulder-width apart and the barbell should be touching the tops of your thighs.

Without moving your upper arm, slowly curl the weight upwards in an arc. Ensure that your wrists remain fixed throughout the exercise.

Pause momentarily at the top and feel the contraction in your biceps muscles.

Biceps curl

Slowly lower to the starting position and repeat for the required number of repetitions.

EXERCISE TIP: This is an easy exercise in which to cheat the weight up. Ensure that you have strict form and that you are not giving the barbell any momentum by moving your upper body.

TRICEPS EXTENSION

PURPOSE: This exercise is the opposite of the previous one. The triceps extension develops the muscles on the back of your upper arm (the triceps). Your triceps muscles are

worked a lot during technical descents when your arms are used to absorb the impact of the trail.

PROCEDURE: Stand in front of a triceps extension machine. Take hold of the bar with a shoulder width grip and with both elbows flexed.

Keeping your upper arm parallel to your body, slowly extend your arms down towards the floor.

Pause momentarily in the fully extended position and feel the contraction in your triceps muscles.

Slowly return to the start and repeat for the required number of repetitions.

Triceps extension

EXERCISE TIPS: Only allow your elbow to bend to 90°.

To isolate the triceps muscles, keep your elbows tucked in to your sides.

SIT-UPS

PURPOSE: Sit-ups develop your stomach muscles (abdominals). As we have seen, mountain biking does not work the abdominals much and as a result they are

comparatively weak. This exercise brings these muscles up to par and helps improve posture.

PROCEDURE: Lie face-up on a comfortable mat. Bend your knees and place your feet flat on the floor. Place your hands on the back of your head.

Slowly curl your torso up to meet your knees.

Pause momentarily in the contracted position, and slowly return to the start.

Sit-ups

Repeat for the required number of repetitions.

EXERCISE TIPS: Keep this exercise ultra slow and focus on your abdominals throughout the whole exercise.

Keep your lower back on the floor at all times.

SIDE BENDS

PURPOSE: Side bends work the sides of your torso (the oblique muscles). They are important muscles involved in manoeuvring the bike and maintaining correct riding posture.

PROCEDURE: Stand upright with your feet shoulder-width apart. Hold a dumb-bell in your right hand and place your left hand on the back of your head.

Slowly bend over to your right side and feel the stretch.

Return to the start position. After the desired number of repetitions, repeat with the other side.

EXERCISE TIPS: Throughout the exercise, make sure that you bend to the side only and not too far forwards or backwards.

This exercise can be made more intense by holding a weight in your free hand.

Side bends

Power and Strength Phase

Following the conditioning phase, you should make your transition to the power and strength stage. This should coincide with your preparation phases P1 and P2 (see chapter eight) and should last up to 15 weeks. In this phase there is an increase in the number of sets (3 to 5), an increase in weight and a subsequent reduction in the number of repetitions (12 to 8).

It is important to note that during this phase the intensity of the exercise is high and as such there is increased stress on the muscles, tendons, ligaments and joints. Great care must be taken whilst you are performing these exercises as an injury now, so close to the race season, could drastically effect your peak performance. If you feel any discomfort whatsoever, back off and reduce the weight and sets and increase the repetitions. Always employ caution.

You should perform the same circuits as in the conditioning phase with the corresponding changes in exercise intensity and duration. This is a long phase and the exercises can quickly feel repetitive and uninteresting. To prevent yourself from becoming stale and unmotivated vary your training. You can spice up your strength training programme in many ways. The most popular methods include:

1. Alternate your workouts with barbell and dumb-bell exercises;
2. Workout with a training partner;
3. Occasionally visit a new gym;
4. Swap the exercises round;
5. Introduce new exercises to the programme.

Muscular Endurance

For the final three or four weeks of your P2 phase (see chapter eight) it is time to work on muscular endurance. You should follow this programme up to the beginning of your competition or peak phase. The sets during this phase will be reduced back to two and there will be an increase in repetitions (20 to 25) with an accompanying reduction in weight. In order to maximise the endurance of the muscles, rest periods between sets will be reduced to a minimum (30 seconds). Because of the extended duration of the sets and the close proximity of the racing season, the total number of exercises will be reduced. Choose your favourite exercise for each body part and incorporate them into a workout.

During the peak phase there will be a great demand placed upon your body as a result of the racing schedule. The key to success and longevity during this phase is maintenance. A tough strength training regime during this phase could easily facilitate the onset of over-reaching and eventually over-training – which may eventually bring about the downfall of your racing season.

During the race season you should use the muscular endurance programme, but you must always exercise common sense with your strength training during this period. If you have a schedule where there are a lot of race dates in close proximity, back off on your strength training and focus upon recovering fully between each race. If your race calendar depicts that one month there are very few races then it would be prudent to include some strength-maintenance training into your programme.

ALTERNATIVE STRENGTH TRAINING METHODS

For one reason or another, you may not be able to get to a gym to do your strength training. This may be because you are pushed for time, stuck at work, travelling, or on holiday. However, this does not mean that you have to cancel your workout, because it is possible to perform an effective strength workout with little or no equipment.

There is a handy strength training device on the market which I advise every mountain biker to have. It is manufactured by Reebok and is basically a length of rubber cord with a handle at either end. This simple gadget allows you to perform numerous upper and lower body exercises, and when it is combined with supplementary bodyweight exercises such as sit-ups, press-ups, lunges and squats, you can get an effective strength workout done.

Strength Circuit
If you are a youth rider and are avoiding training with weights, or if you just fancy a change from your usual programme, you may wish to perform some circuit training. The following circuit can be performed with no equipment.

PRESS-UPS

PURPOSE: This exercise is a body weight version of the bench press. It develops the large muscles on the front of the chest (the pectorals), the muscles on the front of the shoulders (the anterior deltoids) and the back of the upper arm (the triceps).

PROCEDURE: Lie face down on the floor. Your hands should be next to your shoulders with your palms flat on the floor. Your back should be straight and your feet should be shoulder-width apart.

Press-ups

Keeping a straight back, push yourself upwards until your arms are almost straight.

Slowly lower yourself until the tip of your nose touches the floor, then repeat the procedure.

EXERCISE TIP: Vary your hand position to target different areas. A wide hand-span works the pectoral muscles, whereas a close hand-span works the triceps.

CALF RAISES

PURPOSE: This exercise isolates the calf muscles (gastrocnemius) and is an excellent way to develop their dynamic strength.

PROCEDURE: Stand on your left leg and bend your right leg. You will need to hold onto an immovable object for support.

Now raise up onto the ball of your left leg and feel the contraction in your left calf muscle.

Slowly lower yourself back down and repeat the procedure.

EXERCISE TIP: Remember to do the same number of repetitions for the right leg.

Calf raises

BODYWEIGHT SQUATS

PURPOSE: This is an ideal exercise for developing all-round leg strength. It targets the muscles in the entire lower body, but it is the quadriceps that are affected the most.

PROCEDURE: Stand upright with your feet shoulder-width apart.

Keeping your head up and your back straight, slowly bend your knees until they are parallel to the floor.

Slowly push upwards, back to the starting position, and repeat the procedure.

EXERCISE TIPS: Make sure that your knees stay over, and in line with, your feet at all times.

Do not allow your knees to splay outwards.

This exercise can be made more comfortable if you place a low block of wood under your heels.

Bodyweight squats

SIT-UPS

PURPOSE: Sit-ups develop your stomach muscles (abdominals). As we have seen, mountain biking does not work the abdominals much and as a result they are comparatively weak. This exercise brings these muscles up to par and helps improve posture.

PROCEDURE: Lie face-up on a comfortable mat. Bend your knees and place your feet flat on the floor. Place your hands on the back of your head.

Sit-ups

Slowly curl your torso up to meet your knees. Aim to keep your lower back on the floor at all times.

Pause momentarily in the contracted position and slowly return to the start.

Repeat for the required number of repetitions.

EXERCISE TIPS: Keep this exercise ultra slow and focus on your abdominals throughout the whole exercise.

Keep your lower back on the floor at all times.

LOWER BACK RAISES

PURPOSE: The lower back muscles are crucial in mountain biking in order to maintain correct riding posture.

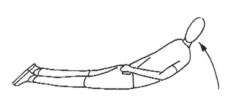

PROCEDURE: Lie face-down on a mat. Place your hands (palms up) on your lower back.

Keeping your hips and legs on the floor, raise your torso as high off the mat as possible.

Lower back raises

Slowly return to the start position and repeat the procedure.

EXERCISE TIPS: Don't strain your neck in the upward phase. Look straight ahead. Hold the contracted position before lowering.

As you become stronger, shift your bodyweight forwards by placing your fingers on your temples.

TRICEPS DIPS

PURPOSE: Triceps dips develop the muscles on the back of your upper arm (the triceps). Your triceps muscles are worked a lot during technical descents when your arms are used to absorb the impact of the trail.

PROCEDURE: Sit down with your back to a bench. Place your palms on the bench, shoulder-width apart and fingers facing forward.

Slowly press your body up and feel the contraction in the triceps.

Slowly lower yourself and repeat the procedure.

Triceps dips

EXERCISE TIPS: This exercise can be made easier by bending your knees.

To maintain tension in the triceps, do not lock out your elbows at the top of the movement.

SIMULATED CHIN-UPS

PURPOSE: This exercise helps develop the large muscles on the upper back (the latissimus dorsi and the rhomboid muscles).

PROCEDURE: Lie face-down on a mat with your arm out to your sides.

Bend your elbows 90°. Raise your arms off the mat and squeeze your shoulder blades together.

Continuously simulate a chin-up movement with your arms.

EXERCISE TIPS: Perform the movements slowly and purposefully.

Simulated chin-ups

Keep the shoulder blade retracted throughout the movement.

You should perform each exercise for one minute and then move immediately on to the next exercise. Once you have completed all the exercises, rest for two minutes then repeat the circuit two more times.

7. FURTHER TRAINING METHODS

HEART-RATE TRAINING ZONES

Just as a machine is composed of smaller, individual working parts, a properly designed mountain bike fitness programme consists of many separate training workouts. Each one of these specific workouts targets a specific area of your fitness and has a crucial, synergistic role in the overall development of your mountain bike fitness.

To ensure that you reach the required intensity to evoke the desired training response, the workout protocols listed in this chapter are accompanied by heart-rate (HR) targets. These targets are individual and are based upon your heart-rate reserve (HRR). In order to calculate your HRR use the following equation:

$$HRR = Heart\ Rate\ (max) - Heart\ Rate\ (rest)$$

This value is then used to calculate your HR target.

$$HR\ (target) = HR\ (rest) + \%\ intensity\ x\ HRR$$

Table 6: Heart-rate Training Zones

% INTENSITY	TYPE OF TRAINING
90+ =	Maximal Training Intensity (MaxTI)
85–90 =	Anaerobic Training Intensity (AnTI)
80–85 =	Aerobic Power (AP)
70–80 =	Steady State Training Intensity (SSTI)
60–70 =	Aerobic Training Intensity (AeTI)
<60 =	Moderate Training Intensity (ModTI)

ANAEROBIC THRESHOLD TRAINING

The area of training that will have the single most profound effect on your mountain bike performance is anaerobic threshold training. But, before we go any further, it is important to have an overview of the different systems that are employed in order to produce the energy that is required for mountain biking. Our energy originally comes from the food that we eat. This nutrient energy is converted, either *aerobically* (with oxygen) or *anaerobically* (without oxygen) into useable energy via our energy systems (see chapter one).

As the intensity of exercise increases and the demand for energy rises, there is a point where the predominant energy system swaps over from the aerobic energy system to the anaerobic energy system, and as a result lactic acid accumulates. The point where this exchange occurs is inter-specific. It is different from rider to rider, but for trained athletes it is typically in the region of 85 to 95 per cent of their maximum heart rate. However, an estimate or prediction falls short of the mark for the serious mountain biker because an error either way can mean the facilitation of fatigue or the failure to attain optimum performance.

Lactic acid is the by-product of anaerobic exercise, but in the presence of oxygen it is metabolised further to yield more energy. As such it is strictly speaking not a waste product. The problem occurs when the oxygen supply fails to meet the demand for energy. As a result, lactic acid production outstrips its rate of metabolism and it begins to accumulate. This is accompanied by a burning sensation in the muscles which is typically associated with performing hard work such as sprints or climbs.

Because the information you require is 'under your skin', the majority of anaerobic threshold tests are invasive. An anaerobic threshold test performed at a sports medicine laboratory involves numerous blood samples to be taken during incremental exercise, which are subsequently analysed for blood lactate concentrations.

Due to the invasive nature, and the equipment required for a laboratory test, it is little wonder that they are expensive and inconvenient. Fortunately there is an alternative method which only requires a resistance trainer and a heart-rate monitor – both of which are prerequisites of the serious mountain bikers' training tool kit.

To meet the demands of increased physical activity, the heart beats more frequently and increases the supply of blood to the working muscles. This vital blood supply transports fuel and oxygen to the working muscles and relieves them of the detrimental toxic by-products. If you graph your heart rate and exercise intensity, it becomes apparent that there is a positive linear relationship between the two. This correlation continues up to a point, then the heart rate levels off despite increases in exercise intensity. This relationship forms the basis of the anaerobic threshold test and can easily be used to determine your anaerobic threshold. The test is advantageous in that it does not require blood samples: it can be performed with minimal equipment and is therefore inexpensive and more convenient than a laboratory test.

Test for Determining Anaerobic Threshold

PURPOSE: The purpose of this test is to ascertain your anaerobic threshold and your corresponding heart rate. This heart-rate information is important because you can use it to determine whether or not you are producing lactic acid at a rate that outstrips your ability to remove it. If you go above your anaerobic threshold you will accumulate lactic acid, which will eventually be detrimental to your mountain bike performance. If you stray too far below it, you won't be accumulating lactic acid, but neither will you be putting in a good performance time. Ideally you should strike a balance between the two.

PROTOCOL: The protocol for the anaerobic threshold test is straightforward and easy to administer. Following a warm-up (see chapter four), commence the test with a starting resistance in the region of 150 watts. There is no exact starting resistance, as this depends on your individual fitness. What might be 'easy' for one rider might fatigue another. If in doubt, err on the side of caution and select a resistance that is too easy. This is preferred over a difficult starting resistance, as the latter will reduce the number of data points. Every minute, increase the resistance, by 10 watts and make a note of the resistance and your heart rate each minute. It is important to maintain a steady cadence throughout the test. You may select your own preferred pedal frequency, but you must maintain this for the duration of the test.

TESTING TIPS: This is a very demanding test, so make sure that you are fully prepared for it both mentally and physically.

Ask someone to assist you with the test and record all of the data. In the interests of safety, it is good practice to have someone at hand especially when you are performing such an intense test.

The next step is to plot the data (intensity against heart rate), either manually or automatically via a heart-rate monitor that is compatible with a personal computer. Connect the points with a straight line, or get your software package to do so, and examine the graph for the point of deflection. Make a note of the corresponding heart rate and power output.

Alternatively you can work with speed instead of power. The protocol of the test remains the same, except that you increase the speed by 1.5 kmh (approximately 1 mph) every minute until exhaustion.

Diagram 5: Anaerobic Threshold Test Performed on a Cycle Ergometer

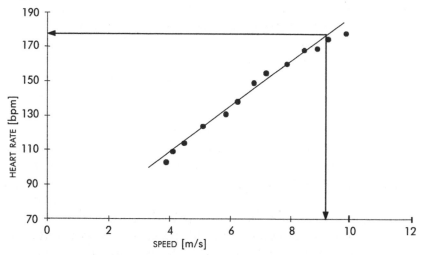

In the above example the rider's heart rate follows a linear pattern as the speed is increased. This relationship continues until a speed of 9 m/s is reached and then, when further increases in speed are performed, the heart rate deflects. For this particular rider the anaerobic threshold is about 177 beats per minute (bpm). In real terms this means that if he exercises at an intensity that raises his heart rate above 177, he will be producing lactic acid which may result in fatigue. If, however, the rider reduces his heart rate significantly below 177 bpm, he will not be exercising at his optimum. The key is to race as close to your anaerobic threshold as possible, rarely going above it for prolonged periods of time.

The effects of training your anaerobic threshold concern these two values. The training effect will increase your heart rate at anaerobic threshold, but only to a certain point, and then it will level out. However, with continued training at anaerobic threshold, you will notice an increased power output at your anaerobic threshold heart rate. In mountain biking terms this means that you will be able to ride at a faster pace before lactic acid accumulates.

Training above your anaerobic threshold requires intense work at high percentages of your maximum heart rate and involves short repeated bouts of intense training punctuated by recovery periods. This type of training is affectionately known as interval training. Before I elaborate on the training protocols for enhancing your anaerobic threshold, I cannot overstate the importance of ensuring that you warm-up and recover thoroughly – more so because of the high intensity and stress that this type of training places on your body.

Time Trial Anaerobic Threshold Test

PURPOSE: The purpose of this test is to ascertain your anaerobic threshold heart rate. It requires very little equipment and is relatively accurate.

PROCEDURE: This test is nothing more than recording your average heart rate during a time trial (10 miles produces an accurate result). By definition, a time trial involves covering a set distance in the quickest possible time. For the test it is important that you maintain a constant speed for the entire time trial. Your average heart rate for the time trial will be within a few beats of your anaerobic threshold.

TESTING TIP: Perform this test as part of a workout and not during a race. The race results will typically give a higher than normal anaerobic threshold as you will no doubt tolerate the accumulating lactic acid more because of the race atmosphere and the flowing adrenaline.

Anaerobic Threshold Workouts (ATW)

The anaerobic threshold workouts are designed to increase your heart rate at anaerobic threshold. When performed correctly they will also increase your power output for a set anaerobic threshold heart rate.

ATW1

PURPOSE: The purpose of ATW1 is to overload your energy systems by working above your anaerobic threshold for extended periods of time.

PROCEDURE: ATW1 is in essence the purest form of anaerobic threshold training. It involves working at a zone that is a few beats above your anaerobic threshold for at least 5 minutes. Build up intensity gradually until you reach the heart rate that is slightly above your anaerobic threshold and maintain it for at least 5 minutes.

WORKOUT TIP: When performing this test it is helpful to have a heart-rate monitor with a training zone facility. Set your alarm to go off when you go above your anaerobic threshold and then try to keep going for 5 minutes.

ATW2

PURPOSE: The purpose of ATW2 is similar to that of the previous workout, except that the workout is more race specific.

PROCEDURE: ATW2 involves simulating a race with your riding partners. You should ride intensely, but ensure that you do not go above your threshold heart rate by more than 5 beats per minute. It is okay to drop a few beats below – in fact you will probably need to – but by the end of the session you should have spent a cumulative 30 to 40 minutes at your anaerobic threshold.

WORKOUT TIP: It can often be difficult to keep track of the intensity at which you are working. There is a distinct advantage having a heart-rate monitor with a memory recall facility, so that you can analyse your training afterwards and make any necessary adjustments for future workouts.

Anaerobic Threshold and VO₂ Max

We first touched on the relationship between anaerobic threshold and VO₂ max in chapter one. As you will remember, VO₂ max is the maximum volume of oxygen that an athlete can absorb and use, and it is often used to assess his fitness. It is argued that anaerobic threshold is a better predictor of athletic performance. This is because the onset of blood lactate accumulation (OBLA) begins at higher levels of oxygen consumption for trained riders than it does for untrained ones. Moreover, as a result of training, you can increase your anaerobic threshold without a commensurate increase in your VO₂ max. Therefore, in this scenario, if you were to measure your fitness in terms of VO₂ max, your test results would indicate that you have not improved, when in reality you have done.

Diagram 6: The Relationship between Anaerobic Threshold and VO₂ Max

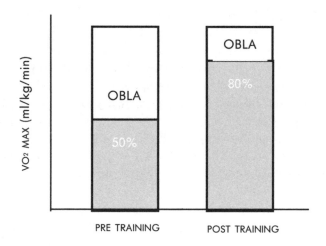

The above graph illustrates the dynamics between VO₂ max and anaerobic threshold for a hypothetical rider. In this situation there is no difference in VO₂ max following training, yet there is a significant increase at the point of OBLA. Therefore anaerobic threshold is a more sensitive measure of the rider's performance.

INTERVAL TRAINING

Interval training is the term given to the mode of exercise which involves performing a series of intense exercise bouts that are punctuated with less concentrated sections, or relief periods. Done correctly, interval training will allow you to perform a greater volume of intense work per training session than if you were to train continually at a similar intensity with no recovery.

Diagram 7: Heart Rate Response to Interval Training

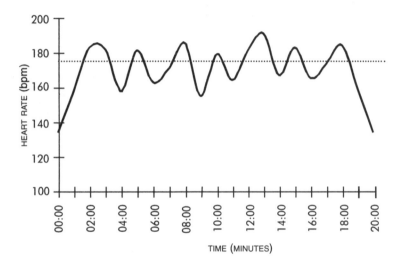

TIME (MINUTES)

Diagram 7 shows a hypothetical interval-training heart-rate response for a mountain biker whose anaerobic threshold is 175 bpm (the anaerobic threshold is represented by the dotted line). In the above example, the cumulative time spent above 175 bpm is greater than that if the rider had ridden intensely from the outset without any rest periods.

In addition, interval training is an excellent tool for increasing speed. Not just riding speed, but also limb speed. In mountain biking, leg speed is closely associated with cadence and pedalling efficiency. Interval training can effectively be used to improve your ability to increase your cadence suddenly, which in turn will greatly improve your ability to accelerate. When your intervals are of short duration, say 30 seconds, there is very little time to move up through the gears; and even if you did have the time, big gears would be cumbersome and would hinder your ability to accelerate. It is therefore an advantage to be able to increase your cadence suddenly and accelerate rapidly in a relatively low gear.

With careful manipulation of the exercise intensity, duration and the relief periods, you can tailor the workout to meet your demands. Intense, short-duration work periods with relatively long relief sections will enhance your explosive speed and your cadence and also develop your phosphocreatine energy system. If you reduce the intensity of the work periods and increase their duration, you will be improving your ability to tolerate hard exercise for prolonged periods of time.

The Workouts
ACCELERATION SPRINTS

PURPOSE: Having the ability to perform acceleration sprints is a very useful resource in your mountain biking repertoire. Acceleration sprints involve increasing your speed from a rolling start, to a moderate fast pace, to a fast pace, all the way up to maximal effort. Acceleration sprints are often required at the end of a race when there is a dash to the line. Here the ability to maintain (and increase) pace over a period of time is of paramount importance if you are to notch up a better finishing position. Quite often during a race you may need to call on acceleration sprints in order to outmanoeuvre a competitor and reach a certain point of the course first. An example of this is beating your opponents to an area of single track where it is then difficult for them to overtake.

PROCEDURE: For this workout you will need a long, flat, off-road section on which to train. You will need to have a 150-metre stretch of ground with plenty of run-off. Approach the 'start' at a relatively easy pace. As you pass the start, change up a few gears and work at a moderately hard pace for 50 metres. Then change up again and ride at a fast pace for the next 50 metres. As you enter the final 50-metre stretch, sprint maximally to the 'finish'. Cycle back to the start at a very easy pace and recover until your heart rate drops to Aerobic Training Intensity (AeTI).

Diagram 8: Acceleration Sprints

WORKOUT TIPS: Before you start, have visual markers to indicate the transition period. Lamp-posts or trees are ideal for this.

When training for acceleration, it is important that you do not think of it in terms of 50-metre 'blocks'. Instead, you should visualise yourself as building up momentum smoothly over a distance until eventually you are working maximally.

In order to allow for progressive overload you can: increase the number of sets (one complete acceleration sprint is one set – perform no more than 10 per workout); increase the distance of each phase; or decrease the rest interval between sets.

HOLLOW SPRINTS

PURPOSE: Hollow sprints train your body to use less effort while sprinting; they teach your body to work in 'economy' mode. This technique can be useful when cycling fast in a bunch of riders.

PROCEDURE: From a rolling start, sprint maximally out of your saddle for 50 metres, then for the next 50 metres sit back in the saddle and maintain your pace and momentum whilst consciously trying to use less energy. Then, for the final 50 metres sprint maximally out of the saddle again. Cycle back to the start at a very easy pace and recover until your heart rate drops to AeTI.

WORKOUT TIPS: Before you start, have visual markers to indicate the transition period. Lamp-posts or trees are ideal for this.

During the middle 50 metres concentrate on pedal technique and relax those muscles not involved in sprinting.

A good technique is to think 'jelly jaw'. If you concentrate on relaxing your jaw muscles, many of the other muscles not involved with sprinting will relax. It is a technique used by world-class 100-metre sprinters and if it works for them, it should work for you.

SPRINT INTERVALS

PURPOSE: Sprint intervals are an excellent way of increasing your tolerance to the build-up of blood lactate that is associated with hard, fast riding. This type of sprinting may be necessary in a race scenario when you are trying to lose a competitor. When two riders are locked in battle like this, it is the one with superior lactate tolerance who is usually the victor.

PROCEDURE: Because this is a high-intensity workout you should warm up thoroughly for about 30 minutes in advance. When you are ready, ride for 2 minutes at Maximum Training Intensity (MaxTI), immediately followed by 2 minutes at AeTI. Recover by riding easy for 15 minutes, then repeat the whole procedure two more times (with a 15-minute cool-down between each set).

WORKOUT TIPS: This is a tough workout, both mentally and physically. Before attempting it you need to be in a fully recovered state and be raring to go.

The workout can be made more interesting by introducing some competition. Have a rider of similar ability train with you. Ride in single file with your training partner about 10 metres behind you. As soon as your partner sees you make your move and initiate the sprint, he has to try to catch up and overtake you within two minutes. Your job, of course, is to out-sprint your partner. For the next sprint, change roles.

DECREASING INTERVALS

PURPOSE: Decreasing intervals train your body to perform a number of repeated maximal sprints with minimum amount of recovery time. In a racing scenario it is a distinct advantage to be able to sprint just as well towards the end of the race as you could at the beginning.

PROCEDURE: Again, this is a high-intensity workout, so you should warm up thoroughly for about 30 minutes beforehand. When you feel ready, sprint as hard as you can for one minute. If you are performing the sprint correctly, you should not be able to maintain the speed for any longer than 60 seconds. Recover and ride easy until your heart rate drops to AeTI. Once this heart rate is achieved, immediately sprint as hard as you can for 50 seconds. Recover once again until your heart rate drops to AeTI and then sprint for 40 seconds, recover . . . and so on until your final sprint is for 10 seconds.

WORKOUT TIP: This is a tough workout, both mentally and physically. Before attempting it you need to be in a fully recovered state and be raring to go.

Because of the rigid timing structure, this exercise lends itself to being performed on a resistance trainer with an assistant to monitor your time.

CLIMBING INTERVALS

PURPOSE: For obvious reasons this workout is really only pertinent to the cross-country mountain biker. During the course of a cross-country race, riders are required to ride hard up short duration hills many times. This is physically demanding and your competitors will cut you no slack. If you can climb well then you will have a distinct advantage over your cohorts. After all, there must be some substance to the old cross-country adage that 'many a race is won on the climbs'. The climbing intervals workout described below is a great way to improve your ability to repeatedly ride hard up tough climbs.

PROCEDURE: Following a thorough warm-up of at least 30 minutes' duration, climb as hard as possible up a hill (no more than 3 km). Don't slow down as you approach the top; instead, try to ride even faster the further you go. Once you reach the top, turn around and ride back down and recover. Keep turning the cranks on the descent in order to keep the blood flowing to your legs. If you haven't recovered by the time you get to the bottom (your heart rate should be near AeTI) do a few loops at the foot of the climb if necessary. Repeat the procedure as many times as you can (no more than 10). As you become increasingly fatigued, you don't have to climb the same height on each repetition. Ride three quarters of the way up, then halfway and so on.

WORKOUT TIPS: Use different climbing techniques, for instance in the saddle and out of the saddle.

Try to go faster, the higher up the hill you get.

Vary your procedure. For instance, on some occasions you may start sprinting in a low gear with a high cadence, and then halfway up the climb, change up (yes up) a gear and then up once more near the top. It's easy to stick with someone on a climb if you are in a low gear: when they struggle and change down, you change up, pull away change up again and power through and over the top of the climb – don't slow down like everyone else.

FARTLEK TRAINING

Fartlek training is a gift to anyone following a long-term training programme as it can often inject a breath of fresh air in an otherwise monotonous regime. Fartlek is a Swedish term which means 'speed play' and was popularised by Swedish Olympic coach Gosta Holmer as an effective training protocol. Fartlek training borrows heavily from the interval style of training, but offers more flexibility and freedom due to the absence of a rigid framework. In other words, the session is informal yet still initiates a training response.

Because of the lack of structure, this form of training is ideally suited to off-road riding. In contrast to interval training, fartlek training is not tied to a structure of pre-determined work and relief periods. Instead the intensity is depicted by the terrain and by you. You ride hard when you are faced with something that requires you to ride hard, like a tough climb or a stretch of fast single-track. And you ride easy when the terrain dictates, for instance when there is a technical section that needs to be ridden slowly, or there is a gentle sweeping downhill.

This form of training allows for the typical long-weekend ride to be slotted into your training plan. Throughout the course of a long mountain bike ride, your heart rate will fluctuate widely. It is highly unlikely that this heart-rate trace will fit into a rigid interval schedule. Fortunately, the concept behind fartlek training acknowledges that there are significant fitness benefits to be had from a random mix of intensities that don't happen to fit into a rigid framework.

This particular form of training is of great benefit to the mountain biker, as it allows for an additional degree of specificity. It can sometimes be difficult to perform precise interval training off-road due to the undulating terrain. You may find with intervals that the time-scale requires you to sprint, but the terrain is a downhill; or that you should be resting but you are on a steep climb. Fartlek training allows you to perform your intervals off-road. You may decide to work hard on the climbs and recover on the downhill, or sprint along sections of single track and coast on the fire roads, or sprint from one tree to the next, then recover and repeat. Throughout the entire workout you should vary the intensity and pace based on how you feel, what the terrain is like, and what you want to accomplish. The permutations are limitless.

However, some caution must be exercised and you shouldn't get too carried away with fartlek training. Unless you know the terrain well, it is easy to work too hard. If you have a scheduled recovery ride with a ceiling-limit heart rate (a heart-rate limit that you cannot go above), it is wise to avoid fartlek training altogether. For instance, you might encounter a prolonged hill which would elevate your heart rate above your threshold, rendering the workout at best useless and at worst detrimental to your performance. The price to pay for the unpredictability of fartlek exercise is that it is often difficult to monitor your training. Ideally you should have a programmable heart-rate monitor so that you can analyse the time spent at various intensity levels afterwards.

It is best to use this form of training towards the end of your foundation phase and during your peak preparation phase, because it is an ideal way to introduce intense intervals into your programme. It's also a good way of putting them into practice off-road. That said, you can perform fartlek training at any time especially if you feel that you are getting into a training rut and want to add a bit of flavour to your workouts.

The Workout

PURPOSE: This workout adds an element of fun to your training. It develops several of your fitness components at once and enhances all of your energy systems.

PROCEDURE: Start off riding easy for 10 minutes (easy intensity). This phase can be part of your warm-up.

For the next 30 minutes, ride up every hill you encounter at an even pace (medium intensity). Try to stay in your middle ring.

After each hill, ride slowly and try to bring your heart rate down to AeTI (easy intensity) for two minutes. This may mean that you have to ride very slowly or even do a track-stand if the terrain won't allow for easy riding.

Ride at an even pace and look out for some natural markers (e.g. trees) that are 50 to 60 metres apart. Then perform six sprint repeats (difficult intensity) with one minute of recovery in between.

Following the sprints, ride easy and try to bring your heart rate down to AeTI (easy intensity) for two minutes. This may mean that you have to do a track-stand if the terrain won't allow for easy riding.

Ride the terrain at race pace for the next 10 minutes (moderate/difficult intensity)

Finish off riding easy for 10 minutes (easy intensity). This phase can be part of your cool-down.

WORKOUT TIPS: You can devise you own workout beforehand or make it up as you go along.

Make sure to include all of the intensities: easy, medium and difficult.

AEROBIC ENDURANCE

For the mountain biker, aerobic endurance is chiefly concerned with being able to maintain a riding pace that is predominantly aerobic. This has two main benefits. Firstly, it trains the aerobic energy system to use fats as its preferred fuel, thereby conserving valuable carbohydrates. Secondly, by the very nature of aerobic metabolism, lactic acid is not produced.

The Workout

PURPOSE: The maximum amount of energy per unit time that you are able to produce aerobically is known as your aerobic power. To a large extent this value is dependent upon your cardio-respiratory and aerobic energy systems. Both of these components can be enhanced as a result of correct aerobic training.

PROCEDURE: In order for aerobic training to be effective, you must exercise within your aerobic training zone. Your aerobic training zone lies within your aerobic and anaerobic thresholds. Your aerobic threshold is the minimum workload that will initiate a training effect – below this there will be no observable adaptations. The ceiling limit is your anaerobic threshold, above which you will predominantly be using your anaerobic energy system and producing lactic acid as a by-product.

WORKOUT TIPS: To calculate the corresponding heart rate use the chart in chapter nine.

The minimum duration of the workout should be one hour. The maximum time spent in this zone is dependent on your fitness and mountain bike discipline. It is not uncommon for ultra-distance riders to train for up to eight hours in this zone.

Aerobic System Test

PURPOSE: You should use this test to ascertain your aerobic power and then use it to monitor the progress of your aerobic system.

PROCEDURE: For this test you will need to use a resistance trainer in a gym, or better still you can set your bike up on an indoor trainer. You should prime your cardio-respiratory system by warming up thoroughly before you commence the test. Then ride for 5 miles at a steady target heart rate which is below your anaerobic threshold. Record the time that it took to complete the distance.

TESTING TIPS: To maintain accuracy, it is important that you stay within a couple of beats of your target heart rate.

You should use the test throughout your training programme to assess your aerobic status. The fitter you are, the quicker your time will be for the given heart rate.

PLYOMETRIC TRAINING

Plyometric exercise is a relative newcomer to the world of physical fitness training. It is a form of training that targets and enhances the fitness components that produce instantaneous power, or sudden bursts of energy – traits that are repeatedly required in competitive mountain biking. Leg power is needed for quick sprints, jumps and quick manoeuvres. As such it is important that all mountain bikers incorporate plyometric training into their training schedules in order to achieve complete development. However, plyometric training is especially pertinent to downhill mountain bikers and dual slalom riders, who need an abundance of muscle power in order to ply their trade.

Plyometric training is based on the principle that a concentric (shortening) muscle contraction is far greater than normal if it immediately follows an eccentric (lengthening) contraction. This is often illustrated using the analogy of a spring. If a spring is stretched it gives a far greater contraction force than if it is not. The same applies to muscles.

Plyometric exercises are easy to do and require little in the way of specialised training equipment.

The Workouts
DEPTH JUMP

PURPOSE: The most widely used plyometric exercise is the depth jump. This basic exercise develops leg power and enhances the contractile properties of the quadriceps muscle.

PROCEDURE: In order to perform the depth jump you will need a sturdy box or bench (anywhere between 40 and 100 cm). Stand on top of the bench and drop down, landing either double or single footed. Bending your knees to absorb the shock causes the quadriceps muscles to quickly lengthen. You now need to contract these muscles as quickly and as powerfully as you can. In order to do this, upon landing, you should immediately jump up, exploding as high as possible. The key word here is immediately. As soon as you touch the floor you should instantly begin your explosive jump upwards.

WORKOUT TIPS: To gain maximum benefit from this exercise you should be aiming to spend as little time as possible in contact with the ground.

If you are a beginner, start out performing two-footed landings. As you progress and become stronger, you can overload further by performing single-footed landings. If you are doing single-footed depth jumps, use a low bench in order to avoid injury.

Plyometric exercises enhance both strength and speed characteristics of muscular contraction and it is possible to place emphasis on either one or the other. The higher you drop down, the longer you will be in contact with the ground. This develops the strength component, whereas a lower height will minimise ground contact time and will develop the speed component more.

Bounding

PURPOSE: This is another classic plyometric exercise that is applicable to mountain biking. The purpose of this exercise is similar to that of depth jumps: to develop leg power and enhance the contractile properties of the quadriceps muscle.

PROCEDURE: In order to perform this exercise correctly and reduce the likelihood of injury you will need to use a flat, relatively soft surface such as grass or a running track. Mark out a start and finish area about 20 metres apart. From the start, perform two-footed bounds towards the finish. Aim to complete the distance with the minimum number of bounds. As with depth jumps, you should try to minimise your contact with the ground. As soon as you land you should be initiating your next bound.

WORKOUT TIPS: To gain maximum benefit from this exercise, you should be aiming to spend as little time as possible in contact with the ground.

If you are a beginner, start out performing two-footed bounds. Then as you progress and become stronger, you can perform single-footed bounds by taking a series of huge lunging strides.

Due to the intense nature of plyometrics, it is important that you act conservatively at all times. Ensure that you wear quality footwear with good shock absorption in the soles, and that you can get good purchase on the ground. The risk of injury is higher than in most other forms of exercise, so warm up, start off easy and gradually build up. A starter session for the above plyometric exercises is as follows:

Depth Jumps: 3 x 8 jumps
Bounding: 3 x 20m of bounding

In between sets it is important that you rest. Give yourself at least 30 seconds' rest between each set, more if you think you need it. Tired muscles will not only respond less to the exercises in a power sense, but they may also contribute to a lack of form which may lead to injury.

As with all other forms of exercise, it is important to remember that you are a mountain biker and that although leg power is a valuable asset it should not dominate your training. When you incorporate this workout into your programme, I suggest that you substitute one weight-training session with plyometrics.

8. PUTTING IT ALL TOGETHER

THE THEORY OF PERIODISATION AND SCHEDULING

So far we have examined the specific training workouts that you can use in order to elicit a training response in a specific area of your fitness. For these workouts to be effective they need to be orchestrated into a training schedule. Reaching peak fitness at the right time is one of the most difficult aspects of training to perfect. To be consistently in top form for a specific event, or series, year in year out, like the professionals are, is no accident. It takes them years of learning, careful documentation and analysis of different exercise schedules in order for them fully to understand and hone their fitness to a peak at the right time.

Every individual is different and as such no hard or fast blueprint exists for guaranteed peak preparation. All is not lost, however, as much research has been conducted in this area and a general pattern has emerged which should enable you to arrive at peak fitness at the right time.

Mountain bike events are externally fixed dates and unfortunately they cannot be rescheduled to suit your fitness status. The only option available is to manipulate your fitness to meet the external demands of the race. The best way to do this is via periodisation, as this provides a focus for your training and brings your fitness components to a peak at the right time.

Periodisation involves splitting the year up into sequential training blocks. The blocks are progressive and are designed to bring the rider to peak fitness for a predetermined point in time. Most top mountain bikers work on a 12-month schedule, with a view to reaching top form during the race season and then maintaining it for as long as possible. You should allow at least 20 to 28 weeks for training before the race season, about 20 weeks for your race season (during which you will be able to peak for a cumulative total of between 4 and 6 weeks), and up to 4 weeks' recovery following your peak. That is a 52-week cycle in total.

For this reason, I will be using a yearly cyclical programme as an example, but you can peak more than once in a year if you so wish. It is important to note that the more frequently you peak the more diminished it will be and the probability of over-training will increase many fold.

A cyclical training programme is one that continually repeats itself with each complete cycle called a 'macrocycle'. The typical mountain biking macrocycle contrasts with the calendar year by starting in the autumn. This allows enough time to reach peak fitness for the competition period which characteristically runs from April through to September. However, if your goal is to compete in a winter series then the principle of periodisation still applies; you will just have shift your training phases accordingly. The macrocycle is subdivided into 'mesocycles', each of which has a specific focus. These are then further divided into 'microcycles' or training weeks.

The number of microcycles in a mesocycle is dependent on the areas of fitness that you are focusing on. Some mesocycles are lengthy in order to allow particular fitness components, such as the cardiovascular system, to fully develop, whilst others are relatively short in duration because they are too intense to be included over a prolonged period without fear of over-training.

Included in the description of each mesocycle are examples of training programmes for both cross-country and downhill disciplines. Initially you can use them as a template to get you started, but as you progress you must tailor your programme to suit your own specific needs and weaknesses.

PHASES MAKING UP THE TRAINING YEAR

Diagram 9: The Mountain Bike Macrocycle

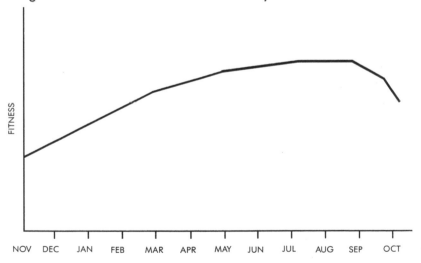

FOUNDATION	PREP 1	PREP 2	RACE SEASON	REST	MESOCYCLES
WEEKS 1 TO 9	10 TO 19	20 TO 29	30 TO 47	48 TO 52	MICROCYCLES

Table 7: The Components of Periodisation

	FOUNDATION	PREP 1	PREP 2	RACE (INC. PEAK)	RECOVERY
DURATION	8–10 weeks	8–10 weeks	8–10 weeks	18–20 weeks inc. 4–6 week peak	4–6 weeks
TRAINING MODE	– off-road – road cycling – running – aerobic cross-training – general sports – technique – resistance trainer	– off-road – road cycling – running – aerobic cross-training – general sports – technique – resistance trainer	– off-road – road cycling – running – aerobic cross-training – technique – strength – resistance trainer	– off-road – road cycling – technique – strength – resistance trainer – racing	– easy light exercise that is enjoyable
TRAINING TYPE	– continuous	– continuous – fartlek – intervals	– continuous – fartlek – intervals	– continuous – fartlek – intervals	– continuous
WORKOUTS	ModTI AeTI SSTI	ModTI AeTI SSTI AP AnTI	ModTI AeTI SSTI AP AnTI MaxTI	ModTI AeTI SSTI AP AnTI MaxTI	ModTI AeTI
PURPOSE	– build base endurance – develop & improve technique	– improve base endurance & develop overall strength – improve technique	– maintain endurance & strength – develop leg power – improve technique – bring all components to a simultaneous peak	– develop peak fitness	– recovery

Foundation Phase

Each new macrocycle begins with developing a base for the rest of the phases to build on. The foundation phase should commence with a battery of fitness tests in order to assess your initial fitness status. The training in the foundation phase is geared to developing your raw fitness which you will subsequently hone and peak for the summer racing. This phase should last for about eight to ten weeks and be skewed towards developing both a solid endurance and a strength base. It also prepares the body for the ensuing phases and will get you back into a training state of mind following the rest and recovery break. A temptation is to underestimate this phase and try to hurry it up by moving onto the more intense training prematurely. Hang fire, for the point to remember here is that training is like a pyramid: the broader the base, the higher the peak you can build. Put the time and effort in at the foundation phase and you will have your highest possible physical peak during the race season.

Diagram 10: Peaking

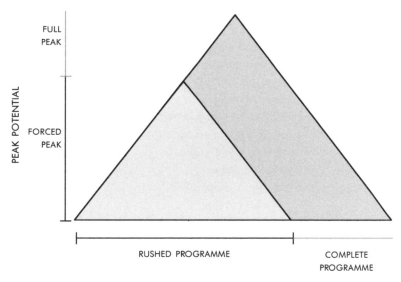

The bulk of your training in this phase should be centred around Moderate Training Intensity (ModTI), Aerobic Training Intensity (AeTI) and Steady State Training Intensity (SSTI) workouts. You should aim to include two high-rep strength workouts per week (no plyometrics at this stage) and a fartlek workout containing some easy climbing. Although you need to initiate a structure into your weekly training, your schedule shouldn't be too rigid at this stage. The race season is still a long time off and it is important not to get too bogged down with training regimes this early on. You need to maintain motivation and have fun, otherwise your enthusiasm will wane several months down the line and your fitness will suffer. You should try to avoid repetitive training by including a lot of cross-training in to this phase. Cross-training involves performing other endurance sports with the aim of improving your base endurance fitness. It also gives your mountain biking muscles a break and prevents you going stale both physically and mentally. For more information on cross-training see chapter thirteen.

Table 8: Cross-country Foundation Phase

MONDAY	Recovery; flexibility (30 minutes)
TUESDAY	1 hour fartlek; strength training (general conditioning)
WEDNESDAY	2 hours endurance ride or cross-training (SSTI)
THURSDAY	30 minutes active recovery (ModTI); flexibility (30 minutes)
FRIDAY	1 hour fartlek (cross-training)
SATURDAY	Strength training (general conditioning); 1 hour endurance cross-training (AeTI)
SUNDAY	2 hours endurance ride (SSTI)

Table 9: Downhill Foundation Phase

MONDAY	Anaerobic threshold workout 1
TUESDAY	1 hour fartlek (cross-training); strength training (general conditioning)
WEDNESDAY	30 minutes flexibility
THURSDAY	Strength training (general conditioning); 1 hour endurance ride (AeTI) or cross-training
FRIDAY	Anaerobic threshold workout 2
SATURDAY	1 hour fartlek; skill work
SUNDAY	2 hours endurance ride (SSTI)

More often than not, the foundation phase will take you through the autumn and early winter months when the chances of catching a cold or illness are heightened. Should you fall ill during this phase, reduce your training volume (to nil if necessary) and only continue with the full programme when you're completely recovered. It is inevitable that we all fall victim to illnesses at some time or other, but there are several actions that you can take in order to reduce the chances to a bare minimum:

1. Bolster your immune system by taking Echinacea. Echinacea is available in tablet form, but is far better when drunk as a tea mixed with a spoonful of honey. Echinacea teas are widely available at all good health food stores.
2. Eat a well-balanced diet and ensure that you are getting enough vitamins and

minerals by consuming plenty of fresh fruit and vegetables. Vitamin C and zinc supplementation has been shown to reduce the severity of colds, but you must catch the cold early for them to have a significant effect.

3. Make sure that you get plenty of sleep. You will need adequate recovery time during this training phase. Any shortcomings with regard to sleep can quickly accumulate and leave you an easy target for illness.

4. Make sure that you eat adequate carbohydrates (see chapter fifteen), as studies have shown that they can reduce the effects of the stress hormones associated with daily life and exercise and thus maintain the strength of your immune system.

5. Try to avoid people who are coughing and spluttering, especially during the high-risk period immediately after you have been training. As an extra precaution get into the habit of washing your hands regularly, as viruses can easily enter the body after you have touched something that is infected.

6. Don't worry about your weight during this period. Rapid weight loss can place a significant drain on the immune system.

7. Work in conjunction with the competing stresses in your life. Wherever possible shun stressful situations and maintain a good, regular training schedule. However, some life stresses are unavoidable and you should reduce your training intensity accordingly. This enables you to accommodate the new stresses and avoid placing too much strain on your immune system.

If you do become ill, all is not lost. As a rule of thumb, if your illness is above your chest – for example as a sore throat or runny nose – then you can test the water by training in the ModTI and the AeTI zones for several minutes. If they clear and your condition improves, you should be okay to continue training, albeit at a lower intensity. If your condition deteriorates, or your symptoms are in your chest, then you should avoid training and seek medical advice. It is foolish to 'push on' at all costs: this will have catastrophic repercussions later on in the macrocycle.

Preparation Phase One (P1)

This phase typically starts around January and should last anywhere between eight and ten weeks. As with the preceding phase, it is important to commence the P1 phase with the same battery of fitness tests in order to review your improvements and highlight key areas that still need work. The training emphasis during this phase is a gradual shift from cross-training to mountain biking. Only at the end of this phase should the volume of time spent training on your mountain bike supersede that spent cross-training. During this period you should also train in the AP and AnTI zones in addition to the ModTI, AeTI and the SSTI that you started in the foundation phase. Towards the end of the P1 phase is an appropriate time to schedule a training camp and focus upon your mountain biking. The training camp should last from one to two weeks and comprise a lot of high-volume work.

This is a relatively demanding training phase, especially if you have included a training camp, and as such it is important to incorporate at least one recovery week in order to allow your body the time to supercompensate and adapt fully to the new strains that you are placing upon it.

Table 10: Example Cross-country Prep Phase One

MONDAY	Rest; 30 minutes flexibility
TUESDAY	2 hours endurance ride (SSTI) with hollow sprints (AnTI)
WEDNESDAY	1 hour fartlek (ModTI–AeTI); plyometrics
THURSDAY	Anaerobic threshold workout 2 (AnTI)
FRIDAY	Rest; 30 minutes flexibility
SATURDAY	Strength training – power and strength; anaerobic threshold workout 1 (AnTI)
SUNDAY	2 hours endurance ride (SSTI/AeTI) with climbing intervals (AnTI)

Table 11: Example Downhill Prep Phase One

MONDAY	Anaerobic threshold workout 1 (AnTI)
TUESDAY	Strength training – power and strength; 30 minutes flexibility
WEDNESDAY	1 hour fartlek (ModTI–AeTI); plyometrics
THURSDAY	1½ hours fartlek (ModTI–AeTI) with long sprints (AnTI)
FRIDAY	Rest; 30 minutes flexibility
SATURDAY	2 hours endurance ride (SSTI/AP) with hollow sprints (AnTI)
SUNDAY	Strength training – power and strength; 1 hour endurance ride (AeTI)

Preparation Phase Two (P2)

This phase has a duration of 8 to 10 weeks, and depending upon your race season it will usually take you from March through to late April or mid-May. Once again, the full battery of fitness tests must be repeated at the start of the phase and you should review your progress to date. The sole purpose of this phase is to bring all of the components of your mountain bike fitness to a simultaneous peak for your racing schedule.

In terms of training volume and intensity, this is the hardest of all of the training phases. You should add MaxTI workouts to your repertoire of training and test your fitness by entering a race that you consider to be of lesser importance than your key races, but nonetheless is of sufficient standard to be a useful

Mountain biking requires a large number of fitness components.

Regular fitness assessment and goal-setting underpin top mountain bike performances.

Correct application of the training principles is necessary for top-level performance.

Turbo trainers are often used during the warm-up before a mountain bike race.

TOP: Thomas Frischnecht shows good climbing fitness.

ABOVE: Sometimes being your own coach means you don't
get the support the professionals do.

TOP: These riders show that women's racing is every bit as exciting as the men's.

ABOVE: A fully laden touring machine can easily add 15 kg to
the weight of the bike. Note the extra water bottles.

ABOVE: Front suspension is widely used in cross-country racing.

LEFT: This rider is making good use of her brakes. Note the two-finger technique.

ABOVE: This rider is using the slow in, fast out cornering technique to good effect.

RIGHT: A plethora of skills are essential for mountain biking. Here riders are preparing for a stream crossing.

TOP: In cross-country events dehydration can be a big problem.
Note the water bottles mounted on the riders' bikes.

ABOVE: Huge demands are placed on every muscle during a mountain bike race.

Mastering which dietary strategies work for you is
essential if you are to perform at your best.

yardstick. At the beginning of this phase, concentrate upon the weak areas of your mountain bike fitness and aim to bring them up to par.

Throughout this phase you should work on the aspects of your fitness that take less time to develop. Depending upon your weaknesses, include:

1. A plyometric workout once a week to increase explosive power;
2. One strength workout per week with lower reps, more sets and increased weight;
3. An increased frequency of intensive endurance workouts and interval work.

Towards the end of this phase is the ideal time to schedule a second training camp. The purpose of this camp is to improve your aerobic capacity and it will be physically demanding. Return from the training camp with several weeks to spare before the start of the race season proper and include a week of active recovery into your schedule.

Whatever the aspects of your fitness you are working on, you should aim to build up momentum in your training which will then spill over into the peak phase.

Table 12: Example Cross-country Prep Phase Two

MONDAY	Rest; 30 minutes flexibility
TUESDAY	2 hours endurance ride (SSTI/AeTI) with decreasing intervals (AnTI/MaxTI)
WEDNESDAY	1 hour fartlek (ModTI–AeTI); plyometrics
THURSDAY	Anaerobic threshold workout 2 (AnTI)
FRIDAY	Rest; 30 minutes flexibility
SATURDAY	Strength training – power and strength; anaerobic threshold workout 1 (AnTI)
SUNDAY	2 hours endurance ride (SSTI/AP) with climbing intervals (AnTI/MaxTI)

Table 13: Example Downhill Prep Phase Two

MONDAY	Anaerobic threshold workout 1 (AnTI)
TUESDAY	Strength training – power and strength; 30 minutes flexibility
WEDNESDAY	1½ hours fartlek (ModTI–AeTI) with decreasing intervals (AnTI/MaxTI).
THURSDAY	1 hour fartlek (ModTI–AeTI); plyometrics
FRIDAY	Rest; 30 minutes flexibility
SATURDAY	2 hours endurance ride (SSTI/AP)
SUNDAY	Strength training – power and strength; 1 hour endurance ride (AeTI) with hollow sprints (AnTI/MaxTI)

Peak Phase

As with the preceding phases, it is important to commence the peak phase with the same battery of fitness tests in order to review your improvements and highlight key areas that still need work.

The mountain bike racing season is undoubtedly a protracted one. In some instances it can be over 20 weeks in duration and it is physiologically and psychologically impossible to be in peak form for that length of time. It is therefore important to ascertain your strategy early on. Most mountain bikers perform the final honing of their fitness during the early race season and only reach their full peak condition towards the end. However the timing of the race, or races, on which you place emphasis will ultimately dictate when you will need to be at your best. The reason for not reaching your full peak fitness at the start of the season is to avoid over-training and the subsequent burnout condition that accompanies this approach. Don't be worried by the prospect of racing when you're not in your best possible condition. If your competitors are smart they will be doing exactly the same. They will be very close to, but not actually in, peak condition. As a result there is no loss of form in relative terms. Those who burn bright at the start of the season will not burn for long; nor will they be doing it again next season!

It is feasible to peak twice for specific races during a single race season, for example the World Cup and the Olympic Games, provided there is sufficient time between them in order to allow for recovery. If you do decide to peak twice in one season, you must be aware that during the mid-race phase you should not be aiming to ride at the best of your ability, despite what your ego says. A periodisation sequence for a double peak should be: Foundation Phase, P1, P2, Peak, Recovery (reduced), P2 (reduced), Peak, Recovery.

If you are aiming to be in peak form only once during the season, you should endeavour to maintain your top form for as long as possible. In some respects you will have to swim against the tide in order to reach this objective. This is because racing brings with it an intensity and ferocity that is unrivalled even in the most severe training workouts. New levels of strain will be placed upon your body as you strive to perform at your best. This strain will cut deep inroads into your reserves and, if left unchecked, may cause you to over-train and burn out unexpectedly.

The key to surviving this phase is to build stages into your microcycles. In order to avoid overloading your body too much, you should not enter more than one demanding race each month. It is also important that you decide, well in advance of the race season, which particular race you want to be in top form for. This may be a regional championship, a national championship, the World Championships or the Olympic Games. However, if you're competing in a race series such as a regional series or the World Cup, your decision may be more difficult. You must tactically ascertain which race in the series would be the most advantageous for you to be at your fittest. This may be dependent on outside factors such as whether or not significant competitors will be racing. Once you have determined the key race of the season, your training should become progressively harder during the build-up to it. Along the way you should train through any other races and make no alteration to your schedule, apart from including a training taper during the week prior to the race and a recovery day the day after it.

You should spend the week after the key race performing active recovery and your training intensity and volume should not exceed SSTI. You should then pick up your normal training schedule and start building up to the next race. It is important to note that this is different from peaking more than once in the season. Here you are not aiming to reach peak fitness several times; rather, your aim is to maintain your peak fitness period for as long as possible and limit the damage caused by racing.

Very few things come close to having a successful race season, especially when you know you have done everything in your power to be in the best possible condition. However, all good things must come to an end and after a hard season's racing you will deserve and, more importantly, *need* a rest.

Table 14: Example Cross-country Peak Phase

MONDAY	1 hour endurance ride (AP); 30 minutes flexibility
TUESDAY	1 hour fartlek; strength training – muscular endurance
WEDNESDAY	Anaerobic threshold workout 2 (AnTI)
THURSDAY	2 hours endurance ride with acceleration sprints
FRIDAY	1½ hours fartlek (SSTI) with climbing intervals – *none if race on Sunday* – (AnTI/MaxTI)
SATURDAY	Rest; 30 minutes flexibility
SUNDAY	Race or anaerobic threshold workout 1 (AnTI/MaxTI)

Table 15: Example Downhill Peak Phase

MONDAY	Anaerobic Threshold Workout 2 (AnTI)
TUESDAY	1 hour fartlek strength training – muscular endurance
WEDNESDAY	Anaerobic threshold workout 2 (AnTI)
THURSDAY	30 minutes flexibility; plyometrics
FRIDAY	1½ hours fartlek (SSTI/AP) with decreasing intervals (MaxTI)
SATURDAY	Rest; 30 minutes flexibility
SUNDAY	Race (AnTI/MaxTI) or strength training – power and strength; 1 hour endurance ride (AeTI)

Recovery Phase

At the end of the race season you should take a break from serious mountain biking and allow your body the time to rest and supercompensate. If you have been following a periodisation schedule all year you will need to unwind from mountain biking, both physically and mentally. For health reasons it is important to stay active during this period, but the intensities of your efforts should be below that of any of the preceding phases. The emphasis during this phase is on active rest and having fun. Do some easy jogging, swimming, walking/hiking, snowboarding, climbing, take a holiday, whatever. If you have become addicted to using a heart-rate monitor during the previous phases, use it during this one to ensure that you're not working too hard.

The recovery phase typically lasts about four weeks, but there is no blueprint as to the exact duration. Keep an eye on your orthostatic heart rate and don't commence the next periodisation schedule until it is within your normal parameters. A good rule of thumb is to perform the alternative sports for as long as you can stand it. When you are champing at the bit to get back into your mountain bike training, that is a good indicator that you are recovered.

YEAR-ROUND RACING

Because it is physiologically advisable that you should only reach peak condition once a year, you may wonder whether or not to race only during that period. It is generally accepted by mountain bike coaches that you should race all season, but not give the same priority to every race.

Racing is an all-important part of the serious mountain biker's training programme. A race can be viewed as a special workout in itself, as it allows you to reach intensities that you would never normally reach during everyday training. Racing also allows you to put all your fitness components back together and get a snapshot of how your training is progressing, and whether the components are working synergistically. It also allows you to become familiar with exercising under great pressure both physically and mentally, and to learn the importance of tactical racing that only experience can teach.

The key to racing during your macrocycle is to ensure that it contributes to your programme rather than upsetting it. You should prioritise your racing and not get hung up on winning every one. As soon as the information is available, write down the races on your calendar and prioritise them. All the races in your peak phase should be where all your attention is focused.

Next there are the races that are important to some extent. A strong field may be present at these meetings, providing an opportunity to compare your fitness with that of other riders. Although you will not be peaking for these events, you should taper your training for three to four days beforehand and increase your carbohydrate intake.

Then there are the least important races, typically the local monthly race. Here you do little more than substitute the race for a workout.

TRAINING CAMPS

The term 'training camp' often conjures up the image of exotic locations that are the preserve of the sponsored rider or the wealthy privateer racer. However this is not necessarily the case, as good deals can often be made with reputable camps if your group number is large enough. Many professional riders jet off to warmer countries with their teams to train and if you are a privateer racer who is able to accommodate the additional expense, then a foreign training camp is ideal. Obviously, southern countries that have a stable climate and appropriate terrain are a distinct advantage. Locations such as Lanzarote, southern France, the Canary Islands, Italy and Spain are all popular areas for mountain bike training camps. However, if your budget won't extend as far as a foreign destination, don't be disheartened as you can still organise a productive training camp in your own country. Make sure that you choose a location where there are low-level hills and a good network of mountain bike trails. You may even find that local mountain bike shops can supply suitable routes that you can use for your training rides.

Training camps afford you the opportunity to remove yourself from your everyday chores and concentrate solely on your mountain bike fitness. You are then able to train hard, eat well and get plenty of quality rest and recovery time. Even if your training camp is in an inclement location, focusing on your training will have an immense impact on your fitness. Ideally you should schedule a training camp late into your P1 and P2 phases and they each need to be of at least two weeks' duration for them to have a significant fitness benefit. Prior to each training camp you should have a relatively easy training week; and following it you may find you need to include a recovery week. During the training camp itself, the majority of your training volume should comprise working at intensities in the SSTI, AP and AnTI zones, with the objective of improving your base endurance and aerobic power. Overleaf is an example schedule for a two-week training camp. Please note that this is only intended as a template and you should adjust your schedule according to your individual requirements.

Table 16: Example Training Camp Schedule

DAY 1	Arrival; 1 hour road ride (SSTI) – *optional*
DAY 2	3 hours road ride (SSTI/AP); flexibility
DAY 3	4 hours road ride (SSTI/AP); flexibility; massage
DAY 4	4 hours fartlek mountain bike (SSTI/AP) with intervals (AnTI); flexibility; massage
DAY 5	Recovery; active rest (ModTI)
DAY 6	4 hours road ride (SSTI/AP); flexibility; massage
DAY 7	5 hours fartlek mountain bike (SSTI/AP) with intervals (AnTI); flexibility; massage
DAY 8	6 hours road ride (SSTI); flexibility; massage
DAY 9	Recovery; active rest (ModTI)
DAY 10	5 hours fartlek mountain bike (SSTI/AP) with intervals (AnTI); flexibility; massage
DAY 11	6 hours road ride (SSTI); flexibility; massage
DAY 12	Recovery; active rest (ModTI)
DAY 13	6 hours road ride (SSTI); flexibility; massage
DAY 14	4 hours mountain bike (SSTI); flexibility; massage; depart

At first appraisal this training schedule may appear very intense. That is because it is. Your training volume at the camp is higher than at any other time in the mesocycle, but it corresponds with one of the few times that you will be devoid of any other stresses except those imposed on your body by your training. As a result you should have plenty of time to ensure that you are fully recovered between workouts.

As you can see, the majority of the training at the camp is performed on the road. For these training sessions you can use a road bike, or simply fit slick tyres to your existing mountain bike. If the latter is your preferred choice then it is advisable to take two sets of wheels with you: one set fitted with knobblies and the other set with slicks. This reduces the hassle of having to remove and refit your tyres in accordance with the workout. For mountain biking, it can be argued that road cycling is contrary to the specificity principle. However, your goal during the training camp is to improve your base endurance and aerobic power by overloading your cardio-respiratory system. This system is ignorant of the mode of exercise that overloads it, whether it is road cycling or mountain biking. The advantage of road cycling during the training camp is that it doesn't stress your whole body as much as mountain biking does. If you were to perform a similar training schedule exclusively off-road, the extra stress on your body would accumulate and you would be forced to reduce the frequency, duration, or intensity of your workouts or run the risk of over-training. Road cycling therefore enables you to maximise your time at the training camp and allows you to include more rides into your training schedule.

TRAINING ERRORS

Despite applying a lot of effort and dedication to their training and preparation, many mountain bikers repeatedly make severe training errors that hamper their performance. The most common mistakes that you should avoid are listed below:

1. TRAINING TOO INTENSELY This tends to occur in the foundation phase and during periods in the macrocycle when there is a need for recovery or low intensity work. The training intensities that naturally suffer are the ModTI, AeTI, and sometimes even the SSTI zones. It is therefore imperative that a heart-rate monitor is worn during these lighter training sessions in order to ensure that the upper heart-rate limit of the zone is not being exceeded. If an intensity is selected that is above the target zone then a completely different fitness component is being overloaded. This type of error does not allow for sufficient recovery, and chronic repetition of this mistake will quickly lead to an unbalanced fitness state and the possible problems associated with over-training.

2. IGNORING PERIODISATION The mesocycles that comprise a macrocycle are progressive. They are dependent on the previous cycle and form the basis of the next. Each mesocycle is of equal importance. A common training error typically made by (although not exclusive to) novice racers is they tend to shorten the early phases of the macrocycle. They rush through the foundation phase and P1 phase in a bid to get to the more glamorous P2 and Peak phases. As a result, they have not fully prepared themselves for the subsequent intense workouts and the structural integrity of the macrocycle soon breaks down. Chronic fatigue and over-training is usually the outcome of this approach.

3. UNDERESTIMATION OF LIFE STRESSES Occupational demands and daily chores place demands on our reserves just as training does. At times, your life stresses may be higher than usual and if you don't take this into account by reducing your training volume then you will not be allowing for full recovery.

4. NOT CONSUMING ENOUGH CALORIES It is important that calorie consumption matches the calories expended during training. If a negative energy balance occurs (not consuming enough food) then something will have to give. Once again the strain is borne by your reserves and can result in a suppressed immune system and reduced fitness. During the foundation phase and the P1 phase, where a suppressed immune system can be catastrophic to

your training, you should err on the side of caution and eat a little more than you actually need. Being two or three kilograms overweight during this period is insignificant to your overall training plan. As the race season approaches, allow yourself plenty of time to get back to your normal racing weight. A rapid loss in body weight has the same negative repercussions as not eating enough.

5. NOT APPLYING THE VARIETY PRINCIPLE An uninteresting training plan will lead to poor-quality workouts and a stagnant state of fitness both physically and mentally. Try to make your workouts interesting. Use different training rides, have different training partners, or go to new locations. Do whatever it takes to make your training enjoyable.

BEING YOUR OWN TRAINING COACH

The vast majority of world-class mountain bikers have their own training coach. As partners they work together, planning and structuring training sessions, with the overall goal of improving the rider's performance. In an ideal world, you too would have your own trainer because a good coach is a valuable fitness asset (please note the word 'good', because in most instances a bad coach is worse than not having one). However, that is the ideal world. In the real world it may be impractical for you to have your own trainer. The three main reasons why mountain bikers don't have a personal coach are:

1. Good mountain bike coaches are not as prolific as those in other sports;
2. Finding a compatible coach can be a difficult task; and
3. Once found, they don't come cheap.

If for whatever reason you don't have your own coach, all is not lost. With the correct skills and knowledge, you can improve your mountain bike performance by becoming your own trainer. In order to do this you will need to do the following:

1. DEVELOP GOOD TIME-MANAGEMENT SKILLS Now that you have assumed the role of coach as well as mountain biker, you are going to have to manage your time efficiently. You will have to design your training programme, perform all of the workouts, assess them and then make any necessary alterations. In the early stages this will be a laborious task and will take up a lot of your time. But as you become more experienced, both as a mountain biker and as your own coach, the whole process will become a lot quicker.
2. SEEK ADVICE OF EXPERIENCED MOUNTAIN BIKERS You should join

the ranks of your local mountain bike club and seek the advice of the most experienced members. Ask them to watch you train and race and see if they can give you some pointers on how you can improve. You should exercise caution here, though, because as soon as you start asking for advice you will be surprised how many armchair experts there are who think they know best. Listen to the advice and weigh it up. If it makes sense try it for a while and then reassess your performance to see if the intervention has had a beneficial effect. Under no circumstances should you follow any advice blindly, even if the most successful mountain biker in your area has given it to you in good faith. Remember, what works for one mountain biker can be detrimental to another.

3. BE ABLE TO ASSESS YOUR PERFORMANCE OBJECTIVELY This is easier said than done. It is a difficult yet highly valuable skill to develop. If you are to get the most from your training, you are going to have to master the skill of being able to stand back from your training and view the whole picture objectively. For instance, if your performance has been low recently, is it because you are working too hard, or because you've been training too little? You will have to differentiate between the two.

4. RELIGIOUSLY KEEP A TRAINING DIARY A detailed training diary is an excellent source of retrospective information. If, for example, you have regularly logged your orthostatic heart rate, this information may allow you to answer objectively the question posed above.

5. KEEP ABREAST OF NEW DEVELOPMENTS IN TRAINING Training theories and methods are always developing and are continuously in a state of flux. Keep on top of these new advances by reading current mountain bike/ fitness magazines and training journals.

What To Do

Your first job as your own coach is to assess your previous training and racing year. Examine the information in your training diary for any areas of concern. Does your training volume affect your performance? Did you suffer from any illnesses? Did you feel run down? Were there any glitches in your training? If so, why? Were there things that you did that greatly enhanced your fitness? What were they? What did you eat on the morning of your best race? All these questions, and more, need to be answered. Any errors, along with any training gems, should be written down at the beginning of your next training diary. They should then be taken into account when you are planning your next macrocycle.

In addition to viewing your training retrospectively, you must also plan your training for the forthcoming macrocycle and for the years that follow. Your long-term racing career should be your overall training concern, which in turn should be broken down into subservient macrocycles. For instance, it would be foolish for a youth-class rider with a weak endurance base to fail to look beyond the next macrocycle. In this example, the rider would also need to bear in mind his long-term goals. It may be prudent for the rider to sacrifice optimal performance this year, in favour of an overall development in his endurance base that will stand him in good stead in future years. Similarly an Olympic mountain biker may wish to forgo races that don't fit into his long-term Olympic plan. It follows, therefore, that before you do anything else you must have a clear overall goal to aim for. For further information on goal-setting see chapter two.

Your next step is to ascertain your current fitness levels and calculate next year's training overload. In most instances an increase in overload of about 10 per cent is a realistic proposition. However, with professional riders who are pushing the envelope of their fitness, the increase will no doubt need to be considerably less. On the other hand, beginner mountain bikers are often capable of making huge gains in their first couple of years of racing and will need to increase the overload accordingly.

Before you begin planning your training year, you should perform a battery of fitness diagnostic tests (listed in chapter two) in order to assess your current fitness status. With this information at hand, you can begin calculating your overload increases and adjusting your new training goals. If you are unsure about the magnitude of the increases in overload, a good starting point is to increase the training strain by 10 per cent as mentioned earlier. In other words, whatever you were capable of doing last year, you should increase it by 10 per cent this year. For example, if you could squat 50 kg for 15 reps last year, you should aim to squat 55 kg for 15 reps this year. Or if last year you could ride a 10-mile, off-road loop in one hour, with an average heart rate of 175 bpm, you should be aiming to ride the same course in 54 minutes with the same average heart rate. Alternatively, riding 11 miles on similar terrain, in the same time and with the same average heart rate would also equate to an overload increase of 10 per cent. It is important to note that the increases are for the same time point in the macrocycle. This means that the increase in overload for your new foundation phase should be 10 per cent greater than last year's foundation phase. It does not mean that you begin your new macrocycle 10 per cent harder than when you left your peak phase, as this would cause a considerable increase in training strain and would no doubt lead to an over-trained condition.

Initially, this new overload may be under- or over-taxing your body. As a result of this it is imperative that, for the first few weeks of the new macrocycle, you pay particular attention to your fitness levels and recovery status. In response to this feedback, you should then make the appropriate alterations to the overload level. With your new training goals and overload levels set, you can now design your macrocycle as described earlier in this chapter.

MONITORING YOUR PERFORMANCE

Even though you have written the blueprint for your yearly training programme, your role as your own coach is not over. On the contrary, it has only just begun. You must assess your fitness throughout the macrocycle and continually evaluate feedback from fitness tests, races, your heart-rate monitor and your own anecdotal feelings.

It is therefore important that you include fitness tests into your overall training plan. You should include these tests at the beginning of each training phase, however they are at your disposal, and you should include additional tests if you feel it is necessary. Fitness tests are demanding, so substitute them for workouts rather than adding them to your microcycle; and only perform them once a month at the most. For further information on fitness testing see chapter two.

Listen to your Body

Correctly assessing your fitness status is a skill. And like all skills, it is slow, clumsy, and methodical in the beginning. In the early stages of assessing your own fitness you will have to rely heavily on fitness tests, heart-rate data and post-race questionnaires. However, as you become more experienced you will be able to read and understand your body with nothing more than intuition. Again this is a skill and needs developing. Riders like Ned Overend rarely use heart-rate monitors, yet they can accurately train within specific zones. They use feedback from their legs, lungs and body sensations in order to adjust their training and assess their fitness. Similarly, some road cyclists talk of being in shape when they can feel a pressure in their legs. This internal feedback is a great skill to have, because it allows you to assess your body on a daily basis, or even during a race, without having to undergo a rigorous testing protocol. On a daily basis you also assess how you are feeling. In your training diary you should record whether you feel tired, hungry, irritable, highly motivated and so on. Over a period of time it may emerge that there is an association between how you are feeling and your training status, or mountain bike performance. These tell-tale signs can then be used to flag up more serious underlying problems in the future that might otherwise have gone unnoticed.

Heart-Rate Monitor Test

The heart-rate monitor test is something you can do every workout. When you are training at different intensities – for instance when you are performing a fartlek session – without looking at your heart-rate monitor try to estimate what the reading is. With practice you can estimate it to within a couple of beats of the actual heart rate.

You should also do this when you are performing your orthostatic heart-rate test in the morning. Without looking, try estimating your heart rate. Associate this heart rate with how you feel at the time. Over time, this relationship between your orthostatic heart rate and how you feel will become stronger. Eventually you will be able to ascertain your recovery status solely by how you feel in the morning.

Prepare for a Change

Even the best-laid plans can go awry from time to time and most training plans need to be adjusted throughout the year. In fact, most programmes on the microcycle level are adjusted routinely and reshuffled in order to accommodate other lifestyle commitments. Your overall training programme should not be written in stone. Instead, it should be flexible and be adapted according to your current fitness status. If you are not getting the performance feedback that you anticipated, you will have to make alterations to your training plan. Small amendments are commonplace and should be no cause for concern. However, if you have drastically to overhaul your macrocycle then something is wrong. You must assess and amend the situation, remembering to write down any mistakes that you have made in order to avoid repeating them next year.

Once you have found a way of training that works for you, you may be tempted to stick with it. On the face of it, this approach sounds like a good idea. But just because a particular type of training works for you, it doesn't mean that there isn't another training method that will work even better. In addition, this particular form of training may be of benefit now, but it might be a completely different story next year. You can't afford to stagnate. This is where being aware of contemporary training methods, theories and nutritional strategies pays dividends. You must not be afraid to experiment with alternative forms of training. Just be sensible. Don't make any drastic changes during an important period in your macrocycle; wait until a less important time to try an alternative training approach. Only make small changes and monitor them closely to assess whether they are proving beneficial or not.

Being a mountain biker and your own coach is difficult. You must guide yourself through the minefield of training and you will no doubt stumble across some steep learning curves along the way. But all of this hard work does come with its own advantages. Although the early years are quite demanding, over time you will increasingly become self reliant. You will develop an enhanced level of knowledge and understanding about how your body works and adapts to specific training methods and nutritional strategies. You will become in tune with your body and have a high level of awareness about its needs. This in turn will lead to fewer alterations to the macrocycle in future years. In addition to all of this, you won't have to worry about whether your coach has got your best interests at heart!

9. SPECIAL GROUPS

All mountain bikers are not equal and as such they should not train the same. Rider stratification is easy to identify at any of the mountain bike races across the country. There are racing categories based on age, experience, ability and gender (see chapter seventeen). Overall the nuts and bolts that underpin the fitness training of these groups are the same, but, depending upon the category, certain considerations need to be taken into account and appropriate changes to the macrocycle should be made.

YOUTH RIDERS

The youth category is probably the most mismatched and uneven category in mountain bike racing. Late developers are pitched against early developers and it is often easy to pick the podium finishers at the starting line by physique alone. Because of this uneven playing field don't put too much stock in your finishing positions. Be more concerned about your own individual performance. This longitudinal approach will be of greater benefit to you and give you a more sensitive gauge on how your own fitness is developing.

If you are a late developer, don't despair – your time will come. Experience has shown that early developers often suffer from motivational problems later on when the mismatched physiques have evened out and performing well is not as easy as it was. The lessons that you learn now, concerning the hard work and the discipline that goes into training will pay dividends later on.

If you're an early developer, you should take heed and not rest on your laurels. It won't be long before those late developers mature and give you a run for your money. Again, be concerned about your own performance rather than comparing it with other riders, as this is the only way you can be sure that you are improving.

Whatever your stage of development, you obviously want to improve your fitness during your macrocycle. Just make sure that you coax the gains rather than force them. Your body is still growing and requires good-quality nutrients and time to recover and improve. You shouldn't train so intensely that the demands placed on your body from your training compete with those from natural growth.

It is therefore important that you keep a close eye on your orthostatic heart rate.

A youth category race typically lasts between 30 and 60 minutes, but what it lacks in duration it makes up in intensity. However, the intensity of the race should not be reflected in your training just yet. You need to mature as a rider and build a sound endurance base first. Your training phases should include a lot of ModTI, AP and SSTI with some interval work. Your longest ride should be for no more than two and a half hours, with the bulk of your rides ranging from an hour to an hour and a half. In order to keep your training interesting and fun, you should vary your programme by performing a lot of cross-training and getting involved in a diverse range of endurance sports.

Technique work should also form a large part of your training and you should work on it as often as you can. Try to ride as wide a range of terrain as possible and include some BMX work in order to increase your bike-handling skills. Avoid including any strength work at this point in your mountain bike career, as the strains of mountain biking and racing are enough for you to cope with for the moment.

JUNIOR RIDERS

The discrepancy between maturation levels are somewhat less in this category and fitness training plays more of a role than in the youth category. This means that you can specialise more in your training.

You should structure your training year according to the periodisation plan outlined previously, but you will need to reduce the overall training volume and the frequency of the intense workouts somewhat. Your training volume for the week should be for no more than ten hours. This ceiling limit will ensure that your training doesn't get in the way of your school or college work, and that you get enough rest and recovery for natural growth and maturation.

The bulk of your training should be in the ModTI, SSTI and AP, with only a small proportion of your training performed at the higher zones. To maintain your interest levels perform your interval work during a fartlek workout and train with a riding partner of equal ability. At this stage in your mountain bike career you can include a one-week training camp and also some strength work. Keep the strength work in the general conditioning phase and perform no more than two of these workouts per week.

As with the youth category riders, you should aim to improve any deficiencies in your riding technique and develop a plethora of skills on varied terrain to the extent that they become autonomous. It is also important that you get first-hand experience of what it is like to compete in a mountain bike race. So, every month substitute one of your regular workouts for a race and analyse your performance afterwards. Where were your strengths and weaknesses? Did you prepare correctly for the race? You'll soon learn that it's not all about brute force and going like a rocket from the starting gun. It's about pacing yourself, riding a smart tactical race and being ergonomically aware. I can wax lyrical about this at length, but the best way to learn this is to do it.

MASTERS/VETERANS

With an increasing frequency in endurance and ultra-endurance sports, older athletes are performing to a standard which is within inches of world-class performance. On an individual level, more and more riders are improving, not deteriorating, with age. The increased occurrence of these anomalies and their contradictions with long-held beliefs have caused sports scientists to ask some potent questions. For example, can exercise override the effects of ageing? And if so, for how long can an athlete expect to continually improve with age?

When it comes to ageing and exercise there are two polar schools of thought. One theory draws a parallel with the human body and a machine. If it is over-used it will become 'worn out' at a quicker rate than if it is not used. This is a bit like preserving a classic car by keeping it garaged all week and only taking it out for a drive on Sundays. At the other end of the continuum is the belief that the body will only improve, and that the ageing process will only be lessened, through *regular* exercise and use.

Anecdotally, both theories have intuitive appeal. Regular exercise promotes sports performance, whilst too much of a good thing can lead to the downward spiral known as over-training. Amongst the ambiguity of findings some hard facts have risen to the surface. What has emerged from gerontology research is that after about 30 to 35 years of age physiological changes occur in all of the body's systems, causing a deterioration of athletic performance which is commensurate with age. This typically includes a reduction in flexibility, aerobic capacity, cardio-respiratory efficiency, maximum heart rate and muscle mass. The only factors shown to increase with age are, unfortunately, reaction time and body fat percentage – not a pleasing thought!

This deterioration in potential is inevitable. However, it seems that the rate at which it occurs need not be as significant as was once thought. Contemporary research is indicating that the ageing process can be offset by the application of an appropriate training programme.

There are two categories of mature competitive mountain biker. Firstly, there are riders who have been physically fit all their life and are aiming to maintain their current fitness level, or at least lessen the rate of its decline. Secondly, there are riders who have remained sedentary for a significant period of time and are aiming to improve their fitness. Studies have shown that it is possible to improve as you get older. This is because it is only your potential that is being curtailed by maturation not your current fitness status. So, provided you aren't already at your full potential there is still room for improvement.

The first step in the process of attaining your mountain bike potential is to accept that you are older and cannot perform or train like the younger riders. Instead of comparing your fitness with how you used to be, you should compare it with how you are now. Start your macrocycle off with the battery of fitness tests explained in this book and use that as a yardstick for your future fitness. You may also find it useful to assess your fitness on a global level by comparing your fitness with that of other masters/veterans racers. This does not mean that you should set your sights low; rather, your goals should be realistic and relative to your age group.

In order to improve physically as a masters/veterans rider, you must train like one. As you get older you need to alter your training and approach it from a different angle because you are now dealing with a different kettle of fish. You need to adjust your training so that it takes into account the different demands placed on your body and the effects that ageing has upon it.

Because the older athlete's body takes a little longer to adapt physiologically to exercise, you should begin your periodisation as early as possible and give yourself the maximum amount of time in each phase. The exception to this is the race season, where you should reduce the number of races and limit the duration by 10 to 15 per cent. The time you spend in the foundation phase should be at least ten weeks, more if your endurance base is weak. You should also allow for more recovery time per microcycle than you have done in the past. In the P1 and P2 phases you can achieve this by reducing the number of high-intensity interval workouts per week (around two to three) and increasing the number of recovery rides; or you can include more interval rides (three to four) but work on a microcycle of ten days instead of the customary week. It is also good practice to limit the frequency of your races to no more than once a month, in order to ensure that you are fully recovered between competitions.

It is very important that the older athlete listens to his body and recognises the symptoms of over-training. There is a reduced margin of error for the older rider and he will not bounce back from an intense exercise bout as quickly as a younger rider will. However, it is in this area that mature athletes often have the edge. Experience has taught them a lot about how their bodies cope, and they have come to recognise when to push and when to back off. A training diary is an important tool in the masters/veterans fitness programme. Log as much as you can – hours of sleep, heart rate, performance, mood, and so on – and periodically analyse them to see if there are any emerging patterns or tell-tale warning signs.

One of the characteristics of ageing is a notable loss in muscle mass, strength and power. In order to combat this, you should place a greater emphasis than normal on these three components and train them all year round, even in the foundation phase. Weight lifting or callisthenics (see chapter six and page 179) should be performed weekly in order to maintain muscle mass and bone density. To complement this you should also include sprints and climbs in your fartlek workouts as part of your yearly training programme.

A reduction in joint mobility correlates highly with an increase in the likelihood of injury and as a result older athletes are more susceptible than younger ones to injuries. The older body takes longer to heal and as such flexibility training is more important than ever. You should aim to stretch every day without fail and become as flexible as possible.

In order to improve your fitness you need to give your body all the help it requires. Provide your body with top-quality building blocks and all the time that it needs to rebuild and recover. You can do this by eating a balanced diet with plenty of fresh foods and making sure that you get your full quota of sleep each night. If you feel tired or fatigued, eat well and reduce your training.

Your body adapts to exercise in pretty much the same way as it used to, it just takes a little more time and care. So if you train intelligently, there is no reason why you can't stay fit, or get fitter, as you get older.

FEMALE MOUNTAIN BIKERS

Apart from the world-class events, women's races tend to attract far fewer competitors than the corresponding men's fields. Because of the limited number of entries, many race organisers group the different categories of riders together. The lack of entries does not reflect a drop in the level of competition. Far from it: the women's races are just as exhilarating and competitive as any other mountain bike race you are likely to watch. Fortunately, over recent years the trend for female participation is on the increase, so hopefully it won't be too long before ranks of the female races are in accordance with the men's and the categories will be able to race separately.

The women's races are held on the same course as the men's, but the number of laps is reduced, with most female races lasting between one and two hours. Besides the duration of the event, there is a noticeable difference in skill level between the two genders. This is indicative of a combination of unsubstantial upper body strength and poor technique. Fortunately, as more and more female mountain bikers are entering the sport at the junior level, the discrepancy in skill level should soon diminish.

It is important that female riders focus on both skill and strength work throughout your macrocycle. If possible, perform your mountain bike workouts on as varied terrain as you can. If this is not feasible, consciously pick different lines each time you ride and continually work on your riding technique. Your upper body strength will develop tremendously by riding off-road, but you can facilitate this process by ensuring that you include a couple of strength workouts each week. If you adhere to the strength programme laid out in chapter six you should see an improvement in your bike-handling skills especially towards the end of a race when muscular fatigue sets in and interferes with the correct execution of a skill.

Due to women's race categories often being amalgamated, and the fact that most female mountain bikers train with fit male riders, the majority of women mountain bikers train at an intensity zone that is too high for them. For instance, if elite level male and female riders are training together during a recovery ride, the male rider may be staying in the ModTI zone whereas the female rider may be encroaching on her AeTI. This means that while the male rider is recovering, the female rider is still imparting a training strain on her body and thus not allowing for full recovery. In order to eradicate this problem you should endeavour to train with male or female riders who have a similar ability to your own.

ULTRA-ENDURANCE/ADVENTURE BIKERS

Increasing numbers of cross-country riders are looking beyond conventional races for alternative ways to test their mettle. This demand has led to an upsurge in the number and diversity of ultra-endurance races that are designed to push the competitors to their limits. Extreme races such as the Alaskan IditaSport race, the Xterra off-road Triathlon and the Leadville 100-mile, plus numerous 24-hour races that are now regulars on the mountain bike race calendar, are becoming increasingly popular.

Although ultra-endurance races are physically gruelling and not necessarily appealing at first appraisal, they do bring with them their own unique rewards. Unlike other forms of racing, where competition is rife and there is an omnipresent emphasis on winning and performing well, the accent in ultra-endurance competitions is, for the bulk of entrants, placed firmly on just finishing or surviving the course. With ultras you don't have to be a hero; it is reward enough just to finish and anything else is a bonus.

Physiologically, ultra-endurance competitions are within the fitness realm of the majority of well-trained cross-country mountain bikers if they train accordingly. It goes without saying that physical fitness is a big part of ultra-endurance races, but it is not the whole story. Patience and a dogged perseverance to continue cycling despite being in a deep state of monotonous fatigue, can often be the difference between going the distance and pulling out. Training for an ultra is a two-pronged approach: you must enhance your resilience and mental toughness, while at the same time you must develop your physical fitness.

As the hours go by in a prolonged race, fatigue eventually sets in. It is not only the muscles that are struggling to work, but also the brain. This is because in ultra-endurance races, carbohydrate metabolism often outstrips carbohydrate consumption despite consuming vast quantities of carbohydrate-rich foods. As a result, a state of hypoglycaemia is almost inevitable. Our brains will only use glucose as their fuel source, and a significant drop in blood glucose levels is quickly detected. This prompts the brain to go into conservation mode and it logically attempts to shut down glucose catabolism by reducing power output. Known as central fatigue, this primal function takes a strong mind to override. It is possible to reduce this impact by training your body to use fat as a fuel and thus, to some extent, spare the blood glucose for the brain.

Before attempting an ultra, your training should be geared towards achieving peak health and fitness. There is no point entering an ultra if you are not in top form, since any weakness will undoubtedly be exposed as the race unfolds and may eventually manifest itself as an injury and a DNF (did not finish). Careful planning and preparation is the key.

You should begin your macrocycle as far in advance as possible – preferably 12 months, but if you are already fit then you use a macrocycle of at least 6 months. Your foundation phase should last anywhere between three and six months and it is here that you should concentrate your efforts on achieving basic health and fitness and establishing a sound endurance base. This is a long phase, so vary your training a lot and take advantage of the diversity of cross-training. Your efforts should be focused in the ModTI, AeTI, and the SSTI, but as you come towards the end of the foundation phase include some AP workouts. Your training volume during this period should be between 12 and 15 hours per week, with one of your rides lasting between 6 and 8 hours. During these long rides, experiment with different types of foods and energy drinks and make notes on which types of foods or combinations work the best. You should incorporate at least two strength workouts per week into your schedule and follow the phases described in chapter six. This is a large volume of training and will need a reciprocal amount of recovery time. During this stage you need to keep other stresses in you life to a minimum. Easier said than done I know, but it is important in order to avoid over-training. At the end of the P1 phase you should take a week off training and perform some active rest exercises. However, if you are already 'mountain biking fit' with a solid endurance base, you can skip the foundation stage and start your training in the P1 phase.

Your P1 phase should last a further two to three months and it is here where you can increase your AP workouts and introduce some AnTI and sprint work. During this period you should focus on increasing your body's ability to use fat as the main energy substrate. In order to become an efficient 'fat burner' you need to increase the amount of fat mobilising and metabolising enzymes within your body. Fat must be transported to the working muscles and this takes time. For this reason, you should start your workouts off easy, allowing time for the fats to be mobilised and transported to the muscles. Start off too quickly and you'll be burning your precious carbohydrates. Slowly build up over a period of 30 minutes to just below your anaerobic threshold and spend at least 30 minutes in this zone. In order to coax your body into metabolising fat you need to consume high-quality fat (please note that this does not mean you should consume high volumes of fat). Animal fats should be avoided at all costs for health reasons. Instead you should source your fats from fish oils (salmon, mackerel) and vegetable oils (extra virgin olive oil and flax seed oil). During this phase you should also be training to become a more efficient rider. You must put in some hard rides, aimed at improving your aerobic power, and include some interval work above anaerobic threshold. Ergonomic riding is a key ingredient to ultra-distance mountain biking, so you should spend a lot of time working on your riding technique.

The P2 phase is a continuation of the preceding phase and should last for two to three months. At the end of this phase all your fitness components should be honed and peaked in preparation for the event. Throughout this phase you should increase the volume of interval work in your microcycle and shift the emphasis of your strength workouts towards improving muscular endurance. Your training should become event specific and, where possible, it should mimic as closely as possible the conditions of the race. Most ultras take place in hostile environments, either in the heat, at altitude, or in extreme cold. Towards the end of this phase is a good time to include a training camp in an environment similar to that of the competition, so that you can acclimatise and get used to riding in the adverse conditions.

All of this training and competing inevitably takes its toll on your body and can quickly drain your reserves. The biggest mistake to avoid when competing in ultra-endurance races (and it is true for all races) is participation in too many – such an easy trap to fall into. The sense of well-being that comes from being in top condition, coupled with the euphoria of finishing an ultra-distance race, may lead you to feel that you are superhuman. The knee-jerk reaction to this is to want to do more and more of these extreme races while the going is good. This is a quick-fire road to disaster and can facilitate a premature ending to your ultra-endurance career. To prevent over-training and burnout, I recommend that you do no more than two ultra distance races per year.

MOUNTAIN BIKE TOURERS

Off-road touring is an exhilarating side branch of the sport of mountain biking. It ranges from a long weekend ride in a local National Park to an epic trip spanning several months and many countries. Whatever the duration, a touring expedition usually requires a lot of preparation and attention to detail. You will need to spend endless hours pondering over what routes to take and which equipment you should carry. And rightly so, but you must also place equal emphasis on attaining the correct physical fitness for your trip. Being fit helps avoid a frustrating mechanical breakdown of the human kind and makes the whole expedition seem less of an effort and thus infinitely more enjoyable.

Training for off-road touring fitness differs from the other forms of mountain bike training in that the goal is not to reach a peak of physical fitness like a cross-country racer would do. Instead, the aim of the tourer is to build up resilience and stamina which will last over a prolonged period. Those who have been touring before will know that the key to being successful lies not in flat-out maximal cycling, but in a slow plod which is around 6 to 8 mph if you are off-road and 12 to 15 mph if you are on-road. This does not mean that touring, or training for touring, is easy. Far from it. Although your body doesn't have to cope with high-intensity effort, it does have to handle long-duration cycling day after day after day. You can be sure that any weaknesses in your fitness, no matter how small, are exposed and magnified to ostentatious proportions after only a couple of weeks of touring. Fortunately, you can get away with the odd fitness weakness if you are only touring for a short length of time. The poor diet and reduced sleep which are often associated with prolonged mountain bike touring, together with the long hours in the saddle, will place an increased demand on your immune system and as such it makes you that bit more susceptible to illness and injury. Being fit is the best way to offset this and the secret to proper touring fitness is to prepare beforehand and then maintain your fitness once you are on the road.

Your first step towards getting fit for off-road touring is to develop a sound endurance base, upon which you can build the rest of your fitness. Because endurance is the major fitness component in off-road touring, you should extend your foundation phase by two to six weeks. Your training should be in the ModTI, AeTI and SSTI zones and you should include a long road ride of around four to six hours' duration once a week. You should do these rides on the same bike that you will be touring on, rather than on a road bike, as this allows you to get accustomed to the riding position for hours at a time. Keep your knobbly tyres on instead of switching to slicks because they will keep your speed in check and prevent you from being tempted to up the ante and ride at a fast pace. The added rolling resistance and slow pace will assist you in staying within your training heart-rate zones. Training on the bike you will be using for touring will also give you the opportunity to make subtle changes to the riding set-up in order to improve comfort and efficiency. Introducing a different touring bike in to the equation at a later date will only complicate matters. Slight changes in riding position will stress your muscles and joints from angles that they are unfamiliar with, exposing them to unaccustomed training strains and thus make them prone to injury. When you are performing these weekly endurance rides, your goal should be to ride for a longer duration each time rather than trying to ride faster.

The P1 phase is a good time for you to get familiar with the weight that you will be carrying on your bike when you are touring. Weigh all of the equipment you are planning to take during your tour, remembering that any fuel or water bottles that you will be using will be full at some stage and will contribute significantly to the overall amount of weight. The typical baggage weight for a long self-sufficient expedition is approximately 12 to 15 kg per person. As part of your training, you should then fit a rack to your bike and simulate this weight with dumb-bell discs; alternatively, you can fit your panniers and fill them with the appropriate ballast (such as house bricks). Use your long-endurance rides to get accustomed to this weight, but keep your early training rides light, then gradually increase the load as you become fitter.

Once a fully laden touring bike is moving on the flat, the cycling is relatively easy. The momentum keeps things going. This is fine until you have to brake sharply, turn suddenly, or encounter a hill. Even the slightest gradient can be energy sapping, never mind the soul-crushing steep climbs. It is on these climbs that your body is stressed the most and it is usually the knees and the lower back muscles that are the first casualties. It is therefore imperative that you include hill work in your training, not as a specific interval workout, but as part of your regular training rides. Try to choose prolonged climbs over severe ones and, as ever, start easy and build up.

Injury is an omnipresent risk when touring. Surprisingly, not all touring injuries occur whilst riding; many are the result of pushing or manoeuvring a heavy bike. Just turning a laden bike around whilst walking requires a lot of upper body strength. During the P1 phase you should perform two strength training workouts per week and adhere to the phases described in chapter eight.

After about ten weeks in the P1 phase it will be time for you to progress to the P2 phase. Unlike the mountain bike racer, there is no need for you to include any

MaxTI training zones or a large amount of interval work as they will be of little use to you. The AP and AnTI training zones will be of benefit and so you should include one of each per microcycle.

At some stage during your tour you will probably come across an off-road hill that will be impossible to ride with all the extra weight you are carrying. Unfortunately, the only way you will be able to overcome the problem is to push your bike to the top. Pushing a heavy bike requires a strong upper body coupled with powerful legs. The off-centre action of pushing a bike uphill places lateral strains on your joints. In order to prevent injury under these circumstances, you will need to develop a balanced musculature that provides support and structural integrity to your joints. Taking into account the specificity principle of training, you should include some hill-push repeats into your P2 phase. Perform six sets of short hill-pushes once a week – to maintain muscle balance you should push from alternative sides of your bike. This phase should be your last training phase prior to your expedition. However, when training for an extended touring trip it is important not to exhaust yourself in your training beforehand. It is good practice to have a full week off prior to your start in order to rest and recuperate. Of course this week won't be true rest as there will no doubt be a million and one other things you'll have to do before you go away.

Prevention, as they say, is better than cure, and a lot can be done whilst on the road to keep yourself in the best possible shape and minimise the risk of injury. Start the tour off easy with short days in the saddle and then slowly build up the duration as the days go by. Begin each day with a warm-up and some light stretching, especially if you've just spent the night in a cramped tent. A light jog followed by some deep knee bends, shoulder circles, neck rolls and side bends should do the trick. You're aiming to raise your body temperature by 1 to 2°C, which is the equivalent of breaking into a light sweat. Follow this with a light stretching session emphasising the hamstrings and lower back. For the first half an hour or so of riding, take it easy – there is no hurry. Spin an easy cadence and then slowly move up through the gears until you reach your normal touring pace. And of course, if you really don't feel up to it on a particular day, take the day off – you're the boss! Instead, just soak in the scenery and enjoy yourself.

FITNESS MOUNTAIN BIKERS

Mountain biking is an excellent tool for increasing and maintaining fitness. This fact has not gone unnoticed by the increasing number of fitness enthusiasts who have chosen mountain biking as a way to improve their health. The overall goal of the fitness enthusiast is progressively to increase their physical fitness to a desired level and then maintain it. For this reason you will need to design a macrocycle similar to that in the previous chapter, but there will be some distinct changes. Most notably, you differ from the competitive mountain biker in that your goal is not to be in peak form for a specific period in time and perform well at races. Thus a rigid macrocycle is not necessary. Rather, you should maintain the progression of periodisation but be more flexible and put the accent on having fun and enjoying your training.

Most fitness bikers are concerned with either increasing aerobic fitness, or weight control, or both. Since aerobic training and weight management go hand in hand, you should spend a protracted time in the foundation phase working in the ModTI, AeTI and SSTI. Once your basic fitness target has been achieved (usually after about 10 to 12 weeks), you can move into the P1 phase and include some strength work (general conditioning) to create structural integrity and enhance your posture.

Often with the advent of fitness comes the desire to test your mettle. If this is the case and you set yourself a target, such as a mountain bike tour holiday or a mini epic off-road ride, then you should move into the P2 phase ten weeks before the event. There is seldom the need for the fitness mountain biker to graduate to the peak phase, but if your venture is particularly demanding then you should adopt the peak phase into your training.

10. ALTERNATIVE FORMS OF TRAINING

THE THEORY OF CROSS-TRAINING

The standpoint throughout this book has primarily been from that of the specificity training principle. That is to say, specific training initiates specific training responses. On the whole this is true – after all, the best sport for getting mountain biking fit is the sport of mountain biking itself. However there are situations where the specificity principle is not applicable. Typical situations where this is the case include when large volumes of training are required, when boredom needs to be avoided, or when mountain biking is not a practical option. Under these circumstances alternative methods of training that overload your target fitness component are acceptable.

Your body's systems have no concept about the mode of exercise that overloads them. They are governed only by the intensity, duration and frequency of the exercise. For example, if you are exercising at 170 bpm, your heart is not influenced by the type of exercise, be it cycling, running or swimming; instead, it is only concerned with beating 170 times every minute to ensure an adequate blood supply to the working muscles. It follows, then, that your cardio-respiratory system can get the same training effect regardless of the mode of exercise as long as it is kept at the target heart rate for the specified duration. This forms the basis of cross-training and has important ramifications for the competitive mountain biker.

ROAD CYCLING

Mountain biking is a very intense sport in which the whole body takes a pounding from shock absorption, propulsion and manoeuvring. It subsequently requires time to recover and supercompensate. If however, you performed all of your workouts off-road you would have to incorporate a lot more rest days into your schedule in order to allow for adequate recovery. Not to do so would run the risk of over-training. However, you can sidestep this issue and train more frequently by staggering your off-road rides with road rides. Because the overall body pounding is absent from road cycling, your taxed muscles get a rest whilst your heart and lungs get an additional workout.

A further advantage of road cycling is that it allows you to maintain a smooth, steady-state heart rate and thus stay within your desired target limits. This can be very difficult to achieve off-road because the undulating terrain often determines the heart rate. It is therefore very difficult to isolate and train just one component of your fitness when you are mountain biking.

RUNNING

All mountain bikers should incorporate running or jogging into their yearly training programme. When running, you are continually supporting your body weight and working all the time. There is no sitting down, coasting or changing to an easier gear, and as a result it is a very intense form of exercise. Because of the lack of rest you can usually get the same cardio-respiratory training effect in a quarter of the time. This factor comes into its own during the winter months when the dark, cold, wet evenings after work are not the most enthralling times to go for a mountain bike training ride. Rather than try to summon up the enthusiasm to go for a freezing four-hour ride with the additional half-hour spent hosing and cleaning your bike, it is far easier to put your running shoes on and go for a quick lung-busting run. Due to its convenience, running should be a significant contributor to both the foundation and the P1 phases of your macrocycle. In addition, running should be included to a lesser extent all year round as it is not unusual for there to be a degree of running in a mountain bike race. Quite often in a race it is ergonomically more efficient to run with your bike rather than actually ride it. At times you may be forced to make this decision if the conditions are: too muddy, or if you've selected a gear that is too high, or if there is a technical section that is above and beyond your current skill level. Whatever the reason, being able to run economically when you're fatigued will be of great advantage when the going gets tough.

From a physiological perspective, mountain biking only involves concentric (shortening) contractions of the muscles, whereas when you are running the muscles also contract eccentrically – that is, your leg muscles lengthen under tension as they absorb the impact of your bodyweight. For this reason, no matter how fit you are at mountain biking, if you are unaccustomed to running you will always have sore legs for a couple of days after a run. This is normal and should cease after a couple of runs. However you should never dismiss any soreness that lingers because the threat of picking up a running-related injury is a real one. Almost every serious runner has had some form of running-related injury and it is your number-one priority not to injure yourself whilst you are running. Remember the running should be adding to, and not detracting from, your mountain biking fitness.

The single most important thing you can do to avoid a chronic running injury is buy yourself the best quality pair of running shoes that you can afford. Visit your local running specialist shop rather than go to a high-street sports shop, because they will give you expert advice and have a wider range of stock. Some running shops even have a foot scan machine which will analyse your gait and assess whether you are a pronator (rotate foot inwards), or supinator (rotate foot outwards). This will help the shop assistant match you with the correct shoe.

Getting the right pair of running shoes cannot be overstated. If you have got an inadequate pair of trainers you will feel it each time your foot hits the ground, and at around 140 foot impacts per minute that is an awful lot of reminders. You will also need to replace your running shoes on a regular basis; usually after about three or four months. Make sure you do this even if the shoe still has a lot of cosmetic life in it because, if you've been running regularly, the cushioning and absorption properties of the mid-sole will have been lost. There is no need to throw your old shoes out: just assign them lighter duties, such as gym work.

It is advisable to perform most of your running work off-road. Grass and woodland trails are more forgiving than tarmac or concrete surfaces and thus have a less detrimental impact on your bones and joints. As with all new forms of exercise, start off easy and gradually build up. If you're a reasonably fit mountain biker then you should be able to cope with a 30-minute run without any undue complications. You should aim for a smooth-flowing running style with an upright torso and comfortable leg stride. Your elbows should be slightly flexed and your arms should assist you with your striding. As you progress, you should be aiming to build up to running a distance of 10 miles, and as a further injury precaution your weekly running mileage should not exceed 30 miles.

HIKING

Hiking is a great form of cross-training. Because it provides a long-duration, low-intensity workout, it is an excellent way to train the MaxTI, AeTI and even the SSTI zones. If you have the time available, hiking is an ideal addition to both the foundation and P1 phases. It is worth bearing in mind that a day out in the hills is often more demanding than it may first appear. Although the intensity is steady and rarely peaks, the long-duration and cumulative effects throughout the day do place a significant strain upon your reserves. To ensure adequate recovery, it is wise to include only a maximum of one hiking workout a week into your training plan.

As with running, your main priority during hiking is to avoid injuring yourself yourself and jeopardising your macrocycle. One of the biggest causes of chronic injury when hiking is equipment that is poorly set up or incorrect. Before you set off on a hike you must ensure that you have the correct footwear. Good fitting, quality boots are an essential item. In addition, you should check that your rucksack has been adjusted to suit your posture and is not going to cause you any discomfort or misalign any of your joints. If you are in any doubt, seek expert help from your local outdoors shop.

SWIMMING

Swimming is a good choice as a form of cross-training because it is relatively impact free. During a particularly demanding microcycle, or following a training camp, a swimming workout can facilitate recovery by removing stresses from your joints yet still allow you to overload and improve your cardiovascular system. It is worth noting that if you are trying to work within a training zone, your heart rate will be lower than normal because of the hydrostatic pressure the water exerts on your body. The reduction in heart rate is around 10 bmp. However it is different from individual to individual. Ascertain what your own difference is and adjust your training zones accordingly.

If you are a competent swimmer you should be aiming to swim for about 1,000 metres and then build up to no more than 5,000 metres. Your choice of stroke is optional, but if you aren't very flexible in the groin area, or you have a back problem, then avoid the breast stroke and opt for the front crawl technique.

OTHER SPORTS

Feel free to include other sports into your cross-training repertoire. Just bear in mind that they must be of sufficient intensity and duration to initiate a training response. Team sports such as rugby, basketball and football should ideally be avoided because they increase risk of injury. Volleyball, squash, tennis or badminton make ideal cross-training sports to complement your mountain biking.

It is important to note that it is only your cardio-respiratory system that is developing in a way that will be of benefit to your mountain biking. When you are cross-training you may be using different muscle groups to those that you use in mountain biking. Even if the muscle groups are the same they will be getting worked in a slightly different way and from a slightly different angle. Because of this, cross-training is ideal for recovery and variety in the foundation phase, but it should gradually be reduced in favour of mountain bike training by the end of your P1 phase.

11. STAYING HEALTHY

Constantly pushing your body to its limits in order to maximise your mountain bike potential is not without its problems. Wear, tear, inadequate nutrition, poor rest and a whole host of other training faux pas will, if ignored, take their toll on your body. Apart from those injuries which are caused by crashes, very few mountain bike injuries are acute. Rather, they are chronic and build up over a period of time, ultimately manifesting themselves at a later date as an over-use injury.

In order to stay healthy and maintain your hard-earned fitness status, you must learn to recognise the symptoms of chronic injury and be able to differentiate them from the aches and discomfort which are the result of quality, productive training. In the majority of mild cases rest is the best cure. However, this chapter is no substitute for a medical specialist; if the problem persists, you should seek the advice of your doctor.

MUSCLE CRAMP

A cramp occurs when a muscle (or muscle group) goes in to an uncontrolled powerful tetanic contraction or spasm. In mountain biking the most common muscles that cramp are those in the calf, hamstrings and hips. Cramps occur when, for some reason, a muscle refuses to relax. The exact precursor of this is as yet unknown. However there are several factors which are thought to be involved causally.

The electrolytes sodium and potassium play important chemical roles in the proper functioning of muscular contractions. Excessive sweating and dehydration can cause significant deviations of the concentrations of these electrolytes, thus causing a shift from the normal homeostatic balance and resulting in improper muscle contraction. Forcing an unprepared, cold muscle to perform maximal or near-maximal contractions for prolonged periods of time has also been linked to a high incidence of muscle cramping. Low blood sugar levels, muscle damage, and ischaemia (poor blood supply) of the muscle cells have been linked to muscular cramping as well.

Muscle cramps can be extremely painful and relief can be sought by stretching and massaging the affected muscle (see chapter four). While this eases the pain, it does not address the underlying cause. To reduce the likelihood of suffering from cramps in the first place, or if you are particularly prone to getting them, make sure that you:

1. Always warm up thoroughly;
2. Replace any lost carbohydrates and electrolytes, either by consuming a commercially prepared electrolyte drink or by eating foods rich in these minerals such as bananas;
3. Always ensure that you are fully hydrated.

BACKACHE

Backache can be the scourge of any mountain bike ride and can arise for seemingly no apparent reason. One of the most common causes is a poorly set up bike and thus an incorrect riding position. This needs to be rectified at once (see chapter twelve). However, this is less likely to be the case with seasoned racers whose riding position have evolved over time to suit their riding style. In these situations it is usually a case of horses for courses. Whilst the competitive 'attack' position is well suited to races lasting up to two and a half hours, it is not the best riding position for the epic long-duration rides which take up most of the day. The solution is to have a second bike for this type of riding and leave your racing steed for what it is intended.

Similarly, you may only be used to one type of terrain and a change can often cause your muscles to fatigue. It is very common to find riders who have trained hard during the off-season and feel that they are fully prepared for their first race, only to learn that their lower backs 'gave out'. This is because during a race there is a lot of 'honking' out of the saddle, often due to poor gear selection (either because of fatigue or congestion on the course). This style of riding puts a lot of strain on your lower back muscles and if you have not taken this into account during your training then they will quickly fatigue and will be the cause of a lot of pain. This example further highlights the importance of the specificity principle and that your training must reflect how you are going to race. When you are working on hill repeats, practise climbing out of the saddle as well as in it and also include strength-training exercises for your entire waist area (see chapter six).

If you ride a hard trail and are stricken with back pain, your suffering may be the result of cumulative impacts to your vertebrae transferred from the trail via your saddle. This can often be alleviated by fitting a suspension seat-post which helps absorb some of the smaller hits. Also if you train/race with a rucksack-mounted drinking system, this may be the root of the problem. For a couple of rides, go back to using your old bottle, or try a bum bag version of the hydration system and see if the pain goes away.

This is a synopsis of the most common antecedents to back pain. However, it is possible that there may be a more serious underlying cause, for instance postural anomalies. If this is the case, or if the pain persists, you should seek the advice of a medical practitioner or a sports physiotherapist.

DELAYED ONSET OF MUSCLE SORENESS

You will no doubt be familiar with the burning sensation in your legs which accompanies an intense workout. This feeling is quite normal and is the result of an accumulation of lactic acid due to working anaerobically. This feeling is usually transient and diminishes with a reduction in exercise intensity. However, sometimes your legs may feel sore the following day, or even the day after that. If it is particularly painful when you attempt to contract the muscle, or even to just touch it, you will probably be suffering from the condition known as Delayed Onset of Muscle Soreness, or DOMS for short.

The pain is, in part, due to torn muscle fibres, muscle spasms and traumatised connective tissue which are a result of the previous intense exercise bout. This condition mainly occurs in riders who exercise infrequently, are returning from a period of no exercise and picking up where they left off, or when the exercise session is of a greater intensity than that to which they are accustomed. Because DOMS can last several days, it can be an inconvenient interruption to your training session as normal training should not be resumed whilst you have DOMS. To reduce the likelihood of DOMS occurring in the first place, you should warm up thoroughly, never skip workouts, set realistic training levels and coax rather than force your body to adapt to them.

KNEE PAIN

Most joint pain afflicting mountain bikers occurs at the knee. The knee is an impressive joint when it is working properly, but it is one of the worst when something goes wrong and it can take many months, even years, to heal. There are many types of knee problems caused by mountain biking. The causes include: poor flexibility of the hamstring muscles; muscular imbalance at the knee; incorrect riding technique; incorrect cleat set-up; and collision damage. Apart from the latter, all of the above causes tend to be chronic and build up over a long period. The only time you realise something is wrong is when it is too late. It is, therefore, very important not to dismiss the odd twinge or ache. You must get it checked out by a specialist immediately.

When you are riding, the knee joint is rarely fully extended. This means the hamstring muscles are seldom stretched. Consequently there is a loss of flexibility in the hamstring muscles (back of thigh) which causes them to become taut and pull on the back of the knee joint. In order to eradicate this problem, you should always endeavour to incorporate stretching exercises for your hamstring muscles into your flexibility programme (see chapter five). An uneven pull on the knee can also be caused by having excessive hypertrophy in the quadriceps relative to the hamstring muscles. This can be corrected by including exercises for the hamstring muscles.

A poorly set-up bike, especially at the cleat/pedal interface, is often the source of knee problems. As a result of the natural biomechanics of your lower limbs, it is quite likely that, during a complete pedal stroke, your foot does not move in only one plane. It may be necessary for your heel to move laterally in relation to the pedal. If this is the case then you should fit cleats which have a certain amount of 'float' built into them, in order to allow your legs to move naturally and reduce the stresses at your knee.

NAUSEA, DIZZINESS AND LETHARGY

Intense mountain biking can initiate a whole variety of uncomfortable sensations including nausea, dizziness and lethargy. These feelings are often a response to low blood sugar levels. As the hours of a ride go by, fatigue sets in. However it is not only the muscles that are struggling to work, but also the brain. This is because as the ride progresses you are metabolising an increasing amount of carbohydrate. Without adequate carbohydrate loading, cessation of exercise, or carbohydrate replacement, a state of hypoglycaemia (or the 'bonk') is almost inevitable.

The human brain will only use glucose as a fuel, and as blood glucose levels drop as a result of exercise, the brain detects this and goes into conservation mode. It attempts to shut down glucose catabolism by reducing power output, while reducing 'central fatigue'. There are several procedures you can employ in order to reduce this impact:
1. Train your body to use fatty acids from your fat deposits as fuel and thus, to some extent, spare the blood glucose for the brain (see chapter nine).
2. Carbohydrate load prior to your ride (see chapter fourteen).
3. Consume carbohydrates during your ride (see chapter fifteen).

MASKING MEDICATION

In western society we have developed a culture known as the 'medicalisation of life'. In short this means that we readily reach into the drugs cabinet in search of a remedy for, or relief from, even the slightest of ailments. What we are forgetting, when we do this, is that the pain is there for a reason – to let us know that something is wrong.

The world of sport is littered with examples where athletes have taken painkillers to mask injury pain in order to 'play on'. The subsequent effect of this is increased injury trauma and in many cases permanent damage. It is therefore important to determine why you are taking the remedy. If it is to ease discomfort, then that is fine. But you should not, under any circumstances, take it to ease discomfort so that you can continue to ride.

PART THREE

Further Factors Affecting Performance

12. APPLIED ERGONOMICS

- How to conserve energy
- Correct bike set-up
- The role of suspension
- The bunny hop
- Correct pedal action
- Correct climbing technique
- Braking
- Cornering

13. MOUNTAIN BIKE PSYCHOLOGY AND SKILL ACQUISITION

- Motivation
- Anxiety
- Mental training
- The theory of skill acquisition

12. APPLIED ERGONOMICS

HOW TO CONSERVE ENERGY

There is no point spending time and effort increasing your fitness if you are going to squander your hard-earned energy and time due to poor riding technique. Riding skills are acquired through experience, watching the professionals, practice, and through trial and error. Sometimes the learning curve is steep and skills are learned quickly; other times it is a laborious process taking a lot of time to fine tune a movement pattern and get it right. An in-depth discussion of mountain bike skills is beyond the scope of this book. Some may argue that mountain bike skills cannot be learned from text, that the trails are the best teacher. Whatever your viewpoint, the following text concerns skills and tips which save time and energy and thus delay the onset of fatigue.

CORRECT BIKE SET-UP

The set-up of your bike has a dramatic effect on how efficient your mountain biking is. The concept is often disregarded because, as with most things, there is a tendency to resist change. More often than not, a rider's current bike set-up is readily regarded as the correct one, not necessarily because it is efficient, but because it feels good. Of course, being comfortable on your bike is important, but it may only feel comfortable because you are used to it. Before you disregard a change to your bike set-up, stick with it for a couple of weeks so that you can become familiar with it and then assess it objectively.

As the sport of mountain biking has progressed and evolved over the years, the bike set-up for each discipline has become more specific. Function has depicted form, and it is truly a case of horses for courses. In each discipline there exists a trade-off between maximum pedal efficiency and the amount of control the rider has. This trade-off continuum has a road cycle at the extreme end of pedalling efficiency, and, at the other end, a BMX with its excellent handling capabilities. In between these two polar parameters lie the disciplines of mountain biking. Cross-country is skewed towards efficiency at the expense of a little handling, whereas downhill is the exact opposite.

Whatever discipline you practise some generic rules apply when setting up your bike:

1. BE AS ACCURATE AS YOU CAN Small changes to your set-up can have dramatic effects on your performance. Do not settle for your set-up being within a centimetre or two of the optimum position. Keep your tolerances tight.
2. WRITE EVERYTHING DOWN Keep detailed notes on your bike set-up. This may be time consuming now but will save many hours in the future. Keeping a record makes it easier to set up a new bike, or return to the previous set-up if a new one does not work.

Over the years the art of setting up a mountain bike for optimal performance has been filtered down to collating four key measurements. The measurements you should record are as follows (see diagram 11):

1. The displacement from the centre of the bottom bracket to the top of the seat. This should be measured in the direction of the seat tube.
2. The horizontal displacement from the nose of the saddle to the centre of the handlebars.
3. The horizontal displacement from the nose of the saddle to the centre of the bottom bracket.
4. The vertical displacement from top of the saddle to the top of the handlebars.

Diagram 11: Key Set-up Measurements

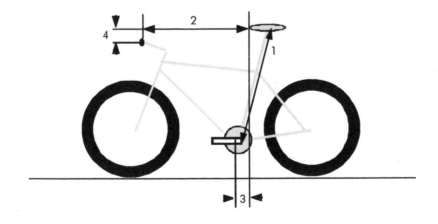

Cross-country Set-up

The cross-country bike set-up should maximise pedal efficiency. It is the shoe-pedal interface where the power transmission occurs, so it is imperative that they are correctly aligned. In order to arrive at the ideal position, you should adjust your cleats so that the ball of your foot is directly over the axle of the pedal. Two further key variables in the pedal efficiency equation are saddle height and saddle fore/aft position. To establish the correct saddle height, sit on your bike with your right pedal in the bottom position. If your saddle is correctly positioned there should only be a slight bend in your right knee when you place the heel of your right foot on the right pedal. If this is not the case, adjust the height of your saddle accordingly. To establish the correct fore/aft position of the saddle, you will need to be in the 'zero' position. This means that when you are sitting on your bike with the crank arm forward and horizontal, a vertical plumb line from your knee should intersect the pedal axle.

The above positions are for maximum efficiency and not necessarily bike handling proficiency. Extreme, technical courses may require a slightly lower saddle height. If this is the case, you will need to readjust the fore/aft saddle position to maintain the zero position.

The horizontal and vertical displacement from the tip of your saddle to the handlebars will dictate your upper body position. This in turn determines where your centre of gravity is. A stretched-out position will bring the centre of gravity forwards and lower, whereas a more upright position will move it upwards and rearwards.

A forward centre of gravity can help stabilise the front wheel on steep climbs, but can be a recipe for an over-the-bars disaster on steep downhills. The stretched-out position can also cause lower back fatigue. A rearward centre of gravity is advantageous on downhills, but can prove a problem on steep climbs if the front wheel becomes un-weighted. Both positions have their advocates and critics, and both have produced champions across the board. You should therefore sample as many different riding positions as possible, make extensive notes and then adopt the one that suits you most.

Downhill Bike Set-up

The nature of a downhill bike and its response to the terrain are ultimately determined by how it is set up. In order to capitalise fully on the performance of a downhill bike, the suspension must be adjusted perfectly so that it is in harmony with both rider and course. It seems that with every season the world of downhill technology is becoming more and more like rocket science. With material and technology advancing at an exponential rate, coupled with trackside feedback from data-logging, any new information on suspension set-up is quickly superseded, rendering it useless. It is therefore not applicable to discuss the intricacies of suspension adjustment in this book. In order to keep abreast of current suspension developments, seek advice from a specialist shop, subscribe to specialist magazines, ask other riders and surf the Internet.

In terms of pedalling efficiency, the zero position also applies to downhill riding. Because the saddle height is traditionally lower in this discipline, you will have to compensate by having your saddle further back on the rails. An upright riding position will move your centre of gravity rearwards, making you and your bike more stable when going downhill.

THE ROLE OF SUSPENSION

Every time you ride over an obstacle on your mountain bike it is accompanied by the obvious upward movement. What is less apparent is the reactive force pushing in the opposite direction to which you are travelling. Newton's Third Law states, 'For every action there is an equal and opposite reaction.' This means that every bump you hit pushes you backwards and slows you down.

Diagram 12: The Effects of Suspension

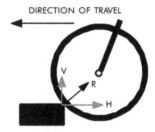

DIRECTION OF TRAVEL

As your wheel strikes an obstacle there is a reactive force (R) which has a vertical component (V) and a backwards horizontal component (H). It is the horizontal component that reduces the forward motion of the bike. If you ride with front suspension, this rearward action is absorbed and minimised, the result being a more economical ride.

THE BUNNY HOP

PURPOSE: The bunny hop is a skill during which the rider un-weights the bike, causing both wheels to leave the ground simultaneously. If you can perform this skill whilst riding at speed, you can use it to clear an obstacle which is in your path.

PROCEDURE: This is achieved by having a relaxed balanced position, with your pedals level and a slight bend in your limbs. Bend your knees and compress your suspension (if you have it), then lightly spring up, maintaining your balanced position and causing the wheels to leave the ground.

SKILL TIP: Timing is essential with this skill, so start easy and build up gradually.

This skill negates any contact with the obstacle and thus avoids any rearward reactive forces associated with riding over obstacles. However, bunny hops cannot be used in all instances (for example on stutter bumps or immediately prior to a corner).

CORRECT PEDAL ACTION

PURPOSE: The interface between foot and pedal can be a source of great energy loss and inefficiency. Correct pedalling motion is a must if you are to maximise your mountain bike potential and minimise wasted effort. For the novice, pedalling is just typically a case of pushing down alternately with each foot, whereas an efficient mountain biker pedals the full circle of each stroke. In order to achieve this, clipless pedals are a must.

Diagram 13: Pedalling Efficiency

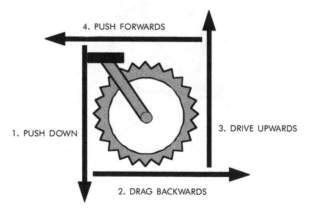

PROCEDURE: In order to maximise your pedalling, you must think of each pedal stroke as comprising four distinct yet seamless phases. The first phase is pushing down on the pedal. Next you should drag the pedal backwards at the bottom of the stroke; this action is similar to scraping something off the sole of your shoe. The third phase is driving your knees upwards. This is followed by pushing your foot forwards.

SKILL TIPS: This can often be a difficult skill to practise whilst riding off-road. Therefore it is best practised whilst training on the road, on rollers or on a turbo trainer.

A good way of enhancing your pedalling efficiency is to perform one-legged cycling drills. As the name suggests, this involves cycling with only one leg at a time, ensuring that you are applying equal force throughout all phases of the stroke.

CORRECT CLIMBING TECHNIQUE

PURPOSE: Climbing steep hills is all too often a source of excess energy wastage. Many riders appear to wrestle the bike up a climb, shifting uncomfortably, whilst top riders seem to conquer the same hill with apparent ease. Immense fitness coupled with good technique is the answer.

PROCEDURE: Steep climbing is a finely tuned balancing act. You must apply enough weight to the rear wheel to ensure that it gets adequate purchase on the ground, whilst ensuring that the front end does not become too light and break loose, causing a loss of control.

Diagram 14: Climbing Technique

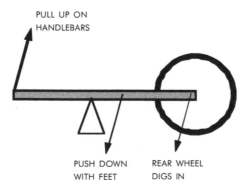

PULL UP ON HANDLEBARS

PUSH DOWN WITH FEET

REAR WHEEL DIGS IN

SKILL TIP: View your mountain bike as a seesaw pivoting around your bottom bracket. If you need to get a purchase with your rear wheel, pull back on the handlebars and push down with your feet.

BRAKING

Each time you squeeze your brake lever you are wasting energy. All the effort that you had put into getting your bike moving you are now wasting by slowing down. Or put another way, you are going to have to apply a whole lot more effort in order to get it moving again, not to mention the time wasted in doing so.

Of course brakes are not a bad thing – in fact they are essential – but they are only useful if they are used at the appropriate time. More often than not a squeeze on the brake lever compensates for a lack of skill and confidence in the given situation. This may help you evade impeding trouble, but in the long run it is inefficient and energy sapping. Practising when and how to brake can maximise the longevity of your glycogen supplies and keep fatigue at bay. Try the following drills:

BRAKING DRILL STAGE 1

PURPOSE: The purpose of this drill is to accustom you to riding without brakes.

PROCEDURE: Find a large expanse of waste land, a disused field, or empty car park and ride around it without using your brakes. Swerve, pick lines and bunny hop over obstacles without touching your brakes. Lean backwards, forwards and sideways and learn how your bike reacts and how you can avoid things purely by manoeuvring yourself and your bike.

SKILL TIP: The first few times you try this you will be grabbing instinctively for your brakes. To avoid using your brakes, point your brake fingers forward and consciously avoid bending them.

BRAKING DRILL STAGE 2

PURPOSE: The purpose of this drill is to take your newly learned skills to a slightly more challenging stretch of single track and see how long you can go without touching the brakes.

PROCEDURE: Making sure that there is plenty of run-out, attempt jumps, drop-offs and corners without using your brakes. This drill further improves your bike handling skills and also your confidence.

SKILL TIP: The first few times you try this you will be grabbing instinctively for your brakes. Again, to avoid using your brakes, point your brake fingers forward and consciously avoid bending them

BRAKING DRILL STAGE 3

Once you are confident with your ability to be at one with the trail, apply the same approach to a gnarly stretch of off-road, or use your skills in a race. Here it is wise to cover the brakes but only apply them when you *have* to, not when you think you might need to.

Most of the world-class racers brake late and brake hard. This limits the amount of time wasted whilst slowing down. They also know the key time to release the brakes in order to quickly accelerate away.

Braking does not just mean slamming on the anchors. There are many subtle manoeuvres you can perform in order to scrub off a little speed here and there. Shifting your weight backwards when you are braking minimises the risk of your rear wheel locking up and skidding. Once again, this allows you to brake late and therefore save time.

Running up banking, dabbing the odd foot, carving into the corners, releasing the brakes early upon exiting a corner, and sitting up proud in order to maximise air resistance are all techniques that can be applied in order to be able to brake late. Experiment with various riding styles to see what works for you.

CORNERING

The way you approach and ride a corner can have a dramatic effect on the ergonomics of your ride. If we use a hairpin bend as an example, the diagram below shows the best racing line in order to maximise exit speed. In racing terms this is affectionately known as the 'slow in, fast out' cornering technique.

Diagram 15: Slow In, Fast Out Cornering Technique

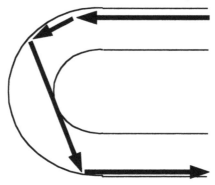

This technique is the product of aiming to exit the corner at the fastest possible speed whilst covering the shortest possible distance. Here you slow down on approach to the corner and make a dramatic turn, clipping the inside of the corner after the halfway point. In doing so, you exit the corner at the maximum possible speed.

13. MOUNTAIN BIKE PSYCHOLOGY AND SKILL ACQUISITION

MOTIVATION

Once you have designed your training programme, your next biggest obstacle is sticking to it. Involvement and improvement to your mountain bike performance should not be viewed as a short-term goal. You can pursue mountain biking for years and you should aim to progress in the long term. However, the progression will only continue as long as there is motivation behind it.

If motivation is the key to sticking with your mountain bike programme, the next logical question is: how can you maintain or improve your motivation levels? Try looking at this question from a different angle and think about what causes your own mountain bike motivation levels to drop. Usually the most common cause is boredom.

The main reasons why boredom creeps into this otherwise exciting sport are:
1. A lack of variation in workouts;
2. Inappropriate or non-existent goals;
3. No structure to the training programme.

Variation
Without variation, any training programme quickly becomes stagnated and leads to a subsequent reduction in motivation. The typical mountain biker, for instance, tends to have a handful of regular routes which he has ridden so many times he could do them in his sleep. Repetitively doing these rides means there are no new stimuli or challenges (save doing it faster) and as such the training programme soon becomes stale. There are many ways that you can introduce variety to your training:

1. REVERSE YOUR USUAL RIDES Reversing the direction of your regular trails is probably the easiest way to double your routes. You will be amazed how different a route is when it is ridden in the opposite direction. What were once gruelling, prolonged climbs are now awesome downhills and vice versa. In

addition you should plan new routes each week and alternate with your training partner whose turn it is. Or for variety you could try riding your regular routes at night, or just use your low-level endurance rides to go exploring for new routes. The only limit is your imagination.

2. CROSS-TRAIN Cross-training is an excellent tool for combating boredom (see chapter ten for details on cross-training). If you were to spend your entire macrocycle mountain biking, by the time the race season came around your motivation for mountain biking would probably have dwindled. You can offset this by including a lot of cross-training in your foundation and P1 phases. This helps you to build a sound endurance base and also prevents your training becoming hackneyed.

3. HAVE A REST One of the symptoms of over-training is mental fatigue and a reduction in motivation (see chapter three). In order to ensure that you are fresh both physically and mentally, you should include regular rest periods in your macrocycle and keep a close eye on your recovery status (see chapter four).

4. PLAN A TRAINING CAMP Including a training camp – especially if it is in a foreign country – into your training is an excellent way to inject some variety into your mesocycle (see chapter eight).

Goal-setting

Without goals there is no point in training. You need to have goals to work towards, and how these goals are structured will have a profound effect upon your motivation levels. Goals that are too difficult will lead to consistent failure, which in turn will stop motivation in its tracks. Goals which are too easy reduce the sense of achievement, which again reduces training drive. It is therefore of paramount importance that you correctly define your goals from the outset. For a more in-depth discussion on goal-setting refer to chapter two.

Structure Your Training

Success breeds success, which in turn increases motivation. If you are to achieve your mountain bike goals then you need a clearly defined plan of how to do it. Chapter eight deals with periodisation and structuring your training in great depth. A hit-and-miss approach to training will only lead to disappointment and a lack of motivation.

ANXIETY

By its very nature, mountain biking (especially downhill) is a veritable breeding ground for fear and trepidation. Woven into the very fabric of the sport are the two classic precursors to anxiety, namely fear of injury and the fear of failure at competition. Both greatly affect how you respond to a given situation and can drastically reduce your mountain bike performance.

Anxiety is an analogue of arousal, where arousal can be defined as our level of activation. It is convenient to view arousal as lying on a continuum ranging from deep sleep to an extremely challenging situation, and to regard anxiety as the negative aspect of arousal. Obviously you need some degree of arousal to participate in mountain biking, because you cannot win races when you are asleep, but you do not want too much. Otherwise you may lose your nerve and ride with excess caution. Somewhere along this continuum is your optimal level for mountain bike performance.

There are not many cases in mountain biking where the rider is under-aroused or not psyched up enough. Nine times out of ten the rider is over-aroused or too psyched up, and is suffering from anxiety. The key to anxiety management is not to wait until it has happened. Instead, you should try to detect the signs early on and deal with them then before they reach epidemic proportions.

Anxiety can rear its ugly head in two forms: it manifests itself mentally as worry; and physically as sweating, trembling and so on. These are termed cognitive and somatic anxiety respectively. More often than not the ringmaster in charge of these two beasts is self-confidence.

Cognitive Anxiety Management

Contemporary sports psychology theories suggest that we are talking to ourselves all of the time. We are not mad; it is just our minds assessing our environment and informing us what is going on. Normally there is no cause for alarm and everything is okay. When we place ourselves in a potentially threatening situation the area of our brain concerned with self-preservation starts talking to us and attempts to initiate some sort of action to deal with the situation to get us out of there. The fight-or-flight response. Therefore, in order to combat worry we need to silence our self-preservation 'voice' and eliminate any negative thoughts we may have.

Thought Stoppage

The first step in the process of eliminating negative thoughts is to be able to recognise them. This is more difficult than it sounds. During the build-up to any race it is commonplace to be concerned with the outcome of the forthcoming event and consequently become anxious. This can start from anything up to a week before the event. Quite haphazardly throughout the day you may find yourself dwelling on the negative aspects of the race, such as 'I am not fully prepared for this race' or 'I am not as good as so and so, who has been doing well this year'. In the absence of thought identification, these cognitions would go by unnoticed and would slowly erode your self-confidence, facilitating the magnitude of the cognitive anxiety that you would endure. Once you become aware that you are having negative thoughts, you can stop them before they become a liability.

Thought Replacement

Once a negative thought has been recognised the next step is to change it to a positive one. Consider the previous thought: 'I am not fully prepared for this race'. You should attempt to change it to: 'I have done all the preparation I can for this race. I haven't missed any of my training and I have been eating a good diet. I should do well'. The other thought, 'I am not as good as so and so, who has been doing well this year,' could be replaced by: 'Sure, so and so has been doing well, but on the last few courses my times have been closer to his and he hasn't been improving. This time I should beat him'.

Thought replacement is a skill, and like any skill it takes time to learn. Executed correctly, a negative thought is immediately replaced by a positive one and as such you constantly have positive thoughts. This state of mind reflects in your race performance.

Improving Self-confidence

Poor self-confidence breeds anxiety. Self-confidence and cognitive anxiety enjoy an inverted relationship: as one goes up, the other goes down. Any technique which enhances self-confidence will automatically reduce cognitive anxiety. High achievers rarely have low self-confidence, so you should allow for achievement in your training programme. A properly designed training programme should have frequent short-term achievable goals. It is important that these goals are not easy to attain, otherwise they will be useless (see chapter two).

Somatic Anxiety Management

The effects of somatic anxiety are probably easier to identify. They are the physical responses to anxiety and include sweaty palms, increased heart and breathing rate, trembling and frequent urination. Whilst cognitive anxiety can start weeks before an event, somatic anxiety usually occurs at the venue. Mountain biking is littered with examples of riders who appear to have a cool persona when they are not at the race, but who get influenced by the buzz of the race scene upon arrival and become a casualty to somatic anxiety. The best way to combat somatic anxiety is to relax.

Somatic anxiety initiates excessive tension in the muscles, which is counterproductive to your mountain biking performance. Relaxation techniques are used to alleviate this tension and calm you, although it can be quite a tricky technique to master initially. Firstly, you must get yourself in a comfortable position, free from distractions, and close your eyes. Then focus on each of your muscle groups. Start at your head and finish at your toes, feeling the tension drain out of them with each exhalation. Once you are completely relaxed, take a few deep breaths and open your eyes. Complete relaxation is difficult to achieve, especially when there are distractions around. You may first have to practise this technique in a quiet place where you won't get disturbed. As you become more proficient at the skill, you will be able to perform it anywhere – even on the start line.

MENTAL TRAINING

Mountain biking is heavily punctuated with roller-coaster examples where riders have excelled at races one week, only to produce a shadow of their performance the following week. Physiologically speaking, very little change can occur in a rider's physical fitness from one week to the next, so there must be an additional influence on performance other than physical fitness alone. I am sure you have had those days where everything flows, where your riding is flawless and your confidence is sky high, and then, for no apparent reason, the next day you are riding like a novice. The good news is you have not suddenly lost your fitness, nor have you lost any of your skills but the bad news is that poor mental fitness is to blame.

Just as you can improve your physical fitness with training, you can improve your mental perspective through training. Mental training enables you to improve your confidence and reduce any anxiety prior to a competition. It also allows you to consolidate skills and re-run the correct lines to take. With all of these benefits it is not surprising that mental training is taken very seriously by the majority of international superathletes; what *is* surprising is that only a handful of mountain bikers are using this amazing training tool to their advantage.

Imagery and Visualisation
Two important weapons in the mountain biker's arsenal, imagery and visualisation, are forms of mental training concerned respectively with the acquisition of skills and the increase of self-efficacy. Both involve imaging a correctly executed mountain bike performance which can take two main forms. You can render the image by: 'seeing' yourself performing the skill as if you were watching yourself on video; or 'seeing' yourself performing the skill through your 'own eyes'. I have put the word 'seeing' in inverted commas because you must not only see the performance, but feel, taste, smell and hear it. Let us use an easy example. Picture yourself lying on a beach and make the image as clear as possible.

Now feel the heat of the sun on your body, add to this the sound of the waves lapping on the beach, the taste of salty air, and the coconut smell of suntan cream. The more senses you use, the more vivid the image becomes.

For both imagery and visualisation it is more beneficial to 'see the image through your own eyes' (mental rehearsal), but many people find the video approach easier to start with. When you perform mental rehearsal, you are in a way 'tricking' your body into thinking it is performing the skill. The more vivid the image, the more your brain is 'fooled'. As the image is being played in your mind, your brain sends impulses to the muscles just as if you were normally executing the skill, only during mental rehearsal the impulses are not as strong and as such do not cause your muscles to move (although they can be recorded on an electromyogram which detects muscular electrical activity). However, your brain is remembering which nerves and muscles it is using and as a result you are learning or consolidating the skill.

The Uses of Mental Rehearsal

1. You can consolidate old skills and learn new ones via imagery.
2. You can run a course accurately through your mind until it is second nature. You know exactly where the tricky sections are and what to do.
3. If you have got a limited amount of time on a course, you can continue practising it in your mind.
4. If you are injured, you can still maintain your current skill level.
5. You can increase your self-confidence and reduce your pre-race anxiety by re-running successful images of yourself on the course.

Correct mental rehearsal is a skill in itself and as such it must be learned. To master this technique fully takes a lot of time and patience, but the rewards are well worth the investment. The ultimate goal is to be able to perform mental rehearsal anywhere. However, when learning the skill it is best to be relaxed and in a quiet environment in order to reduce the likelihood of distractions. Once in a relaxed state you conjure up your desired image using as many senses as possible. The following is a typical example:

> You are sitting on your bike at the start of the course, you have got your right foot clipped in and are leaning on your left leg. You can feel your heart pounding, possibly as a result of having finished your warm-up, but maybe because you are anticipating the race. You feel confident. The air is filled with the sound of gear changes and the smell of GT85. You glance around and see the brightly coloured riders and their shiny bikes. You are looking forward to your race. You spin the cranks round one revolution

with your right foot and can hear the sound of your freewheel clicking. You gently squeeze the grips of your bike and shift your weight slightly on the saddle. A couple of friends walk up and wish you good luck. You nod in recognition, but you are not really paying attention to them. Your thoughts are internal. You remember how successful you were the last time you rode this course. You can feel your confidence well up inside you. You feel relaxed, cool and super strong. You know this is going to be a good race. You know you are going to win.

It is very important that you run the sequence in 'real time' and avoid the temptation of re-running it in slow motion. If you do this you will encounter all sorts of problems when you perform the sequence for real. It follows, therefore, that you do not want to hesitate at any point; instead, you should aim for fluidity and smoothness of your image. When you know the course to this extent your mountain bike performance will flow together and you will appear to do the course without having to think about it – which leaves your mind free to concentrate on race strategies and tactics.

THE THEORY OF SKILL ACQUISITION

Watching the professional mountain bikers ride a course is a joy. The athletic aesthetics can easily fool the casual observer into underestimating the difficulty of the task. The seemingly effortless performance belies the necessary application in training which has to occur in order to achieve such dizzy physical heights.

Each race is a seamless compilation of countless separate skills and it is your ability to collate the appropriate skills that determines whether or not you have good technique. The more skills a rider has, the better prepared he is for different situations that the course may throw at him. A trade-off exists however: he has more skills to search through in order to locate the appropriate one to use, which all takes valuable time. This 'search' time can be reduced to a minimum by practising the skill until it can be performed autonomously, or is what we call 'second nature'. In short, what we are all striving for is a plethora of mountain bike skills which are all second nature.

There are three stages in learning any mountain bike skill. The first one is the novice or cognitive stage, where every movement requires total concentration and is physically exhausting. In this stage, you are constantly having to remember to be in the correct gear, to shift your weight a little here and bend your legs a little there, and as a result your performance is slow, clumsy and inefficient. The final phase is the autonomous stage, where you can do the skill freely without thinking, and with minimum effort. You get there via the second practice, or associative, stage.

Practice is the key. There is nothing new in that, but contrary to popular belief practice does not make perfect. Practice actually makes permanent, which means that if you practise a skill that has flaws in it, that is the one you will learn even though it is not perfect. The key is to ensure that you learn the correct skill.

New skills should be learned when you are not fatigued. Tired muscles work in a less coordinated way than fresh ones and the resultant movement is not worth bothering with, let alone learning. It is easy to spot this at the races: towards the end, some riders have long since lost their style and finesse and they are inefficiently thugging it through to the line. Obviously this physical state is not the best one in which to learn or practise new skills. This does not mean that you should never perform a skill when you are tired. In fact, once you have learned a skill autonomously, try to do it when you are fatigued. Learn new skills early in a workout when you are fresh. Only when you have mastered them should you perform them when you are tired, to make them more robust and less likely to break down under fatigue.

Another rule of thumb for acquiring good technique is to avoid practising it while you are anxious, because that has pretty much the same effect as when you are tired. Transferring this theory onto the dirt means that if you have got to do a six-foot drop-off and you are anxious about injuring yourself, or you are over-conscious about the morbid crowd waiting for you to crash, then don't use this environment to learn the move. The movement will be inappropriate and you will start your learning off on the wrong foot. Instead, remove the stresses when you are practising the skill – this could mean having a go at a smaller drop-off and getting the technique right, or practising on the original one when the crowds are not there. Build up to it and get the technique right on smaller drop-offs before you tackle the big one. Once the move has been autonomously acquired, you should then perform it under stressful conditions so that come race day you are ready for anything the course can throw at you.

Of course, to learn a skill you need something to use as a reference point so that you can copy it. Typically this is watching a professional perform a skill and then going out and practising it yourself. This method usually works well but does have its limitations. The reference point must be fresh in your mind. It is no good powering down a near-vertical descent with a vague idea of how it should be done. You must also be able to view your own performance and objectively compare it with the ideal performance. Sometimes there is a huge disparity between what you think you have done and what you have actually done. It is not unusual for riders whose technique is poor to insist that it was perfect. It can be very difficult subjectively to assess your own skill, especially if you think you are performing it right. Get a rider whose opinion you value to watch your technique and then take on board their comments. Choosing friends to do this is not always a good idea because they will tell what you want to hear for fear of upsetting you. Once you have got this feedback, use it wisely and correct any weaknesses you may have in your technique.

These are the main contemporary theories on learning sporting skills and they all have their place in mountain bike training. However, it must be said that another good method to use is 'trial and error', where you just get out on your bike and have a go. The feedback you get here if it all goes wrong is pain, but the learning curve is a lot steeper!

PART FOUR

Mountain Bike Nutrition

14. FOOD AND DIGESTION

- Calories
- Digestion
- Carbohydrates
- Fats
- Protein
- Calculating calories from the food types
- The energy process

15. DIETARY STRATEGIES AND THE BALANCED DIET

- Manipulating your diet
- Energy drinks
- Water and avoiding dehydration
- Energy bars and gels
- The balanced diet
- Bodyweight management

16. ERGOGENIC AIDS

– Caffeine

– Creatine

– Sodium bicarbonate

– Glycerol

17. YOUR FIRST RACE

– Race categories

– On the day

14. FOOD AND DIGESTION

CALORIES

The nutritional goal central to the competitive mountain biker is to maximise muscle energy output. In the same way that you can get better performance from a car by using better grade fuels, you can also get better performance from your body by using better grade foods. However, the fuel that you put into your car has been refined and is ready to use – unlike the foods that you eat, which have to be refined by your body and converted into usable energy for mountain biking. The SI unit of energy is the joule, but when referring to food the calorie is often used. In this book I will be using the calorie because it is a unit most people are familiar with and it is also the unit that most food manufacturers use on their labels. Within the calorie unit there is much confusion. One Calorie (note the capital C) can also be called a kilocalorie (kcal) which is the equivalent to 1,000 calories (note the lower-case c), and each calorie corresponds to 4.18 joules.

It is also important to note that, in addition to providing energy, your food also supplies the necessary building blocks to enable you to repair yourself after a workout and get fitter. 'You are what you eat,' as the old adage goes.

Once eaten, your food must be broken down into its constituent parts before it can be absorbed and used. All foods are composed of carbohydrates, fats and protein, and each has its own function. Carbohydrates are the predominant energy source during mountain bike competition. Fats will be a major contributor to the energy demands in slower, longer events such as touring or ultra-endurance races. Proteins rarely contribute to the energy equation unless under starvation conditions; however, they contribute greatly to the metabolic processes of the body and also supply the materials for growth and repair.

Not all foods are equal. Different foods contain different percentages of fats, protein, and carbohydrate. Some foods contain greater amounts of energy than others. Because of this, certain types of foods are best suited for certain jobs within the body, while other foods are best avoided altogether. In order to understand fully the role of food in our diet, we first need to look at digestion and the different food types.

DIGESTION

Digestion is the process whereby food is broken down into its constituent parts by mechanical and chemical means. The whole process begins in the mouth where the mechanical action of chewing breaks down the food into smaller pieces. The first stage of chemical digestion also occurs here when enzymes in the saliva begin to act on the food. The food next passes into the stomach, then the small intestines, and is broken down further by churning and additional enzyme activity. The food is then absorbed from the small intestine into the bloodstream and transported to areas of the body where it is needed.

This process obviously takes time and the quicker the absorption rate the more readily available the food is for use. Not all foods are digested and absorbed at the same rate. Some foods, such as fruit, can be ready for assimilation within 40 minutes whereas others, such as fatty red meat, may take the best part of a day and a half! As a rule of thumb: if the food you eat is in liquid form, in low concentration and has a low fat content, and you are resting, then the rate of digestion will be far quicker than if the food is solid, has a high fat content, and you are exercising.

Once the food has been absorbed, it is either used immediately or stored for future use. Each food type is stored in its own way and contributes to your energy output uniquely.

CARBOHYDRATES

Carbohydrates are the most important fuel type for the competitive mountain biker. They should make up the bulk of your diet and contribute around 55 to 60 per cent of your total Calorie intake.

Carbohydrates exist in different forms. The basic component of every carbohydrate is the single sugar unit or monosaccharide. Glucose and fructose are the most common dietary monosaccharides. If these are joined together they form sucrose, a double sugar unit, or disaccharide. Finally, if several monosaccharides are bonded together a polysaccharide or complex carbohydrate is formed, an example of which is starch.

Because of their simple nature, monosaccharides are readily absorbed and provide the muscles with quick energy. Disaccharides first have to be broken down into their constituent monosaccharides before they can be absorbed and utilised, which clearly takes a longer amount of time. It follows that polysaccharides take the longest amount of time to be digested and absorbed and as such are ideally suited for supplying your muscles with slow-release long-term energy.

A well-balanced mixture of each type of carbohydrate will ensure an even supply of energy throughout a race or training ride. Monosaccharides will contribute to the early stages of the race, or when quick energy is needed such as in sprints. The disaccharides and polysaccharides will provide the energy as the race progresses.

Unfortunately for the competitive mountain biker, the amount of carbohydrate stored in the body is limited and is about 360 g. The bulk of carbohydrate is stored as glycogen in the muscles and liver, and there is some glucose present in the blood. Each gram of carbohydrate when fully oxidised can supply a maximum of 4 kcal, so there is about 1,440 kcal (360 x 4) of energy stored in your body in the form of carbohydrates. This is enough to fuel about one hour's worth of racing, which clearly is not enough to supply the energy demands of a typical race. Additional energy comes from the oxidation of fats and from additional carbohydrates consumed during the race, usually in the form of energy drinks or bars.

FATS

Fats tend to get a lot of bad publicity, but for the competitive mountain biker they are an integral part of the racer's diet. Gram for gram, fat provides more energy than any other food type and when fully oxidised each gram of fat can supply a maximum of 9 kcal. Theoretically, the average mountain biker has enough stored energy from fat to complete about three and a half days of continuous mountain biking.

The bulk of the fat (85 per cent by kcal) in our diet is in the form of triglycerides which are used mainly for their energy content and are of the greatest importance to the competitive mountain biker. They consist of three fatty acid molecules attached to a single glycerol molecule. Cholesterol and phospholipids are the fats that make up the rest of our diet and are chiefly concerned with cell growth.

The bulk of fat digestion occurs in the small intestine and involves breaking down the fats into their component molecules. The fatty acid molecules are zippered off the glycerol molecule and are called free fatty acids. These are then transported around the body and used as an immediate energy source if needed, or stored in fat cells for later use.

Fat and the healthy diet
Although fat is an important part of our diet, too much, especially of the wrong type, can be harmful to our health. There are four main types of dietary fat.

MONOUNSATURATED FATS Dietary sources of monounsaturated fats are chiefly vegetable oils, the most common being olive oil.

POLYUNSATURATED FATS Polyunsaturated fats are the least harmful of all dietary fats. They actually increase the levels of good cholesterol (high-density lipoprotein HDL) and reduce the levels of bad cholesterol (low-density lipoprotein LDL).

SATURATED FATS Saturated fats are mainly found in animal fats and dairy products and are typically solid at room temperature. Saturated fats are linked to heart disease because they increase the levels of LDL cholesterol and contribute to atherosclerosis of the arteries and arteriosclerosis.

TRANS FATS Trans fats are man-made fats and are the product of hydrogenating unsaturated fats. Unfortunately, this process makes the trans fat behave like a saturated fat and they cause the levels of LDL cholesterol to rise. A major dietary source of trans fats are biscuits.

    The recommended intake for fats is between 20 to 30 per cent of the total Calorie consumption. From a health perspective it is important that the majority of your fat intake is in the form of polyunsaturated fats. Saturated and trans fats are best avoided whenever possible. Read the food labels carefully.

PROTEIN

Protein makes up the remainder of the diet, which should be between 15 and 20 per cent of the total Calories consumed. Proteins are made up from amino acids (often called 'building blocks') of which there are 20. Of these, 11 can be made by the body and as such are regarded as non-essential. The remaining nine amino acids cannot be synthesised and must be present in the diet. These are called essential amino acids.

    The digestion of protein begins in the stomach and continues in the small intestine. The proteins are broken down into their constituent amino acids, which are then transported to the cells of the body which require them. The amino acids are then used to synthesise the particular protein required by the cell. The main roles of protein within the body are growth and repair.

    Meat and dairy products are good sources of all 20 amino acids. Vegetables also contain certain amino acids, although care and planning is needed to ensure that all amino acids are consumed if you restrict yourself to a vegetarian diet.

CALCULATING CALORIES FROM THE FOOD TYPES

Worked Example #1

To calculate the amount of Calories that come from carbohydrates, fats and proteins in your diet, create a table and list the foods that you have in a day. See below for an example.

Table 17: Foods Consumed in a Day

FOOD	AMOUNT	TOTAL kcals	CARBS (g)	FAT (g)	PROTEIN (g)
Breakfast					
APPLE	1	81	20.25	0	0
TOAST WITH A LITTLE	2 slices	134.3	23.92	1.98	5.20
BUTTER	10g	72.9	0	8.10	0
PURE ORANGE JUICE	8oz	106.16	24.8	0	1.74
Mid-morning snack					
BANANA	1	105	25.08	0	1.17
WATER	16oz	0	0	0	0
Lunch					
VEGETABLE SOUP	1 tin	150	31.5	0	6.00
BREAD	4 slices	268.51	47.84	3.95	10.40
COFFEE	1 cup	5	0.28	0.3	0.28
APPLE	1	81	20.25	0	0
Afternoon snack					
COFFEE	1 cup	5	0.28	0.3	0.28
BISCUITS (DIGESTIVES)	2	196.29	27.77	7.93	3.46
Dinner					
BAKED POTATO	1 large	330	75.53	0	6.97
BEANS	1 tin	267	48.0	3.0	12.00
WATER	16oz	0	0	0	0
Evening snack					
MILK	8oz	121.12	11.71	4.64	8.13
BISCUITS	2	194.49	27.77	7.73	3.46
TOTAL		2117.77	384.98	37.93	59.09

You can obtain the nutritional information from the packaging of your food, or you can get specialised Calorie Counter books, which are well worth investing in.

Because most manufacturers list the carbohydrates, fats and proteins in grams, you must convert these amounts into Calories. To do this you must multiply the total for each food type by the 'Calorie Factor' 9 for fats, 4 for carbohydrates and protein.

	CARBOHYDRATE	FAT	PROTEIN
TOTAL IN GRAMS	384.98	37.93	59.09
MULTIPLY BY	4	9	4
TO GIVE TOTAL IN KCAL	1539.92	341.37	236.36

In order to calculate the percentage kcal from carbohydrates, fats, and proteins we must divide each one by the total kcals for the day and multiply by 100.

$$\frac{\text{Total kcal for food type}}{\text{Total kcal for day}} \times 100 = \% \text{ kcal of food type}$$

Therefore: Carbohydrate = $\dfrac{1539.92}{2117.77} \times 100 = 73\%$

Fat = $\dfrac{341.37}{2117.77} \times 100 = 16\%$

Protein = $\dfrac{236.36}{2117.77} \times 100 = 11\%$

This may seem a rather laborious task, but after only a couple of weeks you will soon develop an 'eye' for carbohydrate-rich food and not have to calculate everything.

Worked Example #2

FOOD – CHOCOLATE BAR

TOTAL CALORIES	256kcal
CARBOHYDRATE	27.8g
FAT	14.4g
PROTEIN	3.8g

Remember: For each gram: Carbohydrate = 4 kcal; Fat = 9 kcal; Protein = 4 kcal

KCAL FOR –   Carbohydrate = 27.8 x 4 = 111 kcal

Fat = 14.4 x 9 = 130 kcal

Protein = 3.8 x 4 = 15 kcal

To calculate % kcal: divide by total kcal and multiply by 100

% KCAL FOR —   Carbohydrate = [111/256] x 100 = 43%
Fat = [130/256] x 100 = 51%
Protein = [15/256] x 100 = 6%

THE ENERGY PROCESS

The term 'energy' is synonymous with nutrition and with regard to mountain biking, it is mainly concerned with the capacity to perform work. As we have seen in chapter one, the nutrient energy 'locked up' in food cannot be used directly by your working muscles. Instead it must be converted to adenosine triphosphate (ATP), by a chemical process called respiration. ATP resynthesis is achieved by three energy systems:
1. Phosphocreatine system;
2. Anaerobic glycolysis;
3. Aerobic glycolysis.

The Energy Demands of Mountain Biking
Before deciding on how much, and of what type, of energy to consume, it is imperative to have an understanding of the energy demands of our sport. In order to set a mountain bike in motion there are resistive forces that must be overcome, all of which require energy. The most significant of these are gravity, friction and obstacles. When you are riding at speeds less than 15 mph, wind resistance is not a major factor, and therefore not a big problem in cross-country mountain biking, but it may adversely affect downhill performance.

The majority of data regarding the energy demands of cycling are based on laboratory tests which are performed under ideal conditions. This means that the environment is unchanging. For instance, it is assumed there is a level road and no wind. This, of course, is a far cry from a mountain bike race; however, we can learn a lot from this information and by extrapolating it we can apply it to mountain biking.

The most striking feature of this type of research is that resistive forces increase as speed increases, and thus more energy is required. A one-to-one relationship does not exist between the resistive variables; in fact, the faster we ride the less efficient we become. During a race, when you are riding at your fastest and most intense, you are also cycling at your least efficient and therefore you must account for this when planning your diet.

In order to ensure that you have an adequate supply of energy for a mountain bike race, you must manipulate your diet to include certain foods at specific times, otherwise you may find yourself in an energy crisis. The main source of energy during a mountain bike race is from carbohydrates. As we have seen, the amount of carbohydrate the average rider can store is only equivalent to about an hour's worth of racing, which in most instances is grossly inadequate.

There is a wealth of scientific studies showing that endurance performance correlates positively to muscle glycogen stores (see diagram 16) and there is also evidence indicating that high-intensity repeated sprint work, similar to that in mountain biking, also suffers from low glycogen reserves.

Diagram 16: Glycogen Depletion and Endurance Performance

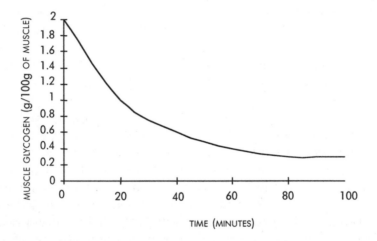

The glycogen stored in the working muscles is used first. Then, once this has been spent, blood glucose is used, which in turn is serviced by liver glycogen stores. Once all the stored carbohydrates are exhausted, fat is then oxidised in order to meet the energy demands of the exercise. This transition of substrate, from carbohydrate to fat, is accompanied by a dramatic drop in pace and, if glucose is not consumed, the rider will suffer from hypoglycaemia and become rapidly fatigued.

It is therefore a distinct advantage to delay the time that stored carbohydrates are depleted. Indeed, this is possible through careful dietary management. The principles of this practice are relatively simple. Firstly, aim to boost stored carbohydrate levels prior to the race/training session. Secondly, supply carbohydrates during the race/training session. Finally, maximise carbohydrate storage following the race/training session in preparation for the next exercise bout.

15. DIETARY STRATEGIES AND THE BALANCED DIET

MANIPULATING YOUR DIET

Pre-race dietary strategy

As suggested in the previous chapter, the depletion of the body's carbohydrate stores can be offset by careful dietary manipulation. Enhancing your muscles' ability to store glycogen can be achieved by using a process called 'carbohydrate loading'. The original, classic loading procedure involved a strict regime whereby riders would severely reduce their carbohydrate intake for several days and then dramatically increase it. The idea behind this process was logical. The initial depletion phase was used to deceive the body into assuming there was a carbohydrate famine. This in turn would cause the muscles to go into glycogen conservation mode and store any carbohydrates that came their way. When performed correctly, this maximal storage situation in the muscle coincided with the dietary carbohydrate increase phase, and the result was a net increase of stored glycogen. Despite significant elevations in muscle glycogen stores, this method is now virtually redundant among most mountain bikers because of the disadvantages associated with the initial low-carbohydrate diet. During the carbohydrate depletion phase, practitioners of this method often reported feeling weak and irritable, as well as having a loss of coordination and a low sense of well-being. Indeed, in some cases athletes have developed 'flu-like' symptoms. These symptoms and feelings are exactly the same as 'hitting the wall', and if you've ever experienced that, you'll know it's not worth repeating, especially prior to a competition.

Instead most athletes now opt for the more user-friendly, modified loading procedure. The protocol for the modified loading procedure is highlighted in diagram 17 (overleaf).

Diagram 17: Modified Carbohydrate Loading Procedure

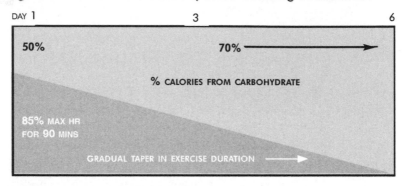

This six-day regimen is relatively easy to follow. On the first day you should ride for 90 minutes at an intensity equivalent to AP (see chapter nine), and then gradually reduce the duration of your daily workouts until day six. For days one to three the amount of calories you get from carbohydrates should be approximately 50 per cent, subsequently increased to 70 per cent for days four to six. Generally, this equates to consuming approximately 10 g of carbohydrate per kg of bodyweight. In other words, if you weighed 70 kg then you would need to consume 700 g of carbohydrate for days four to six. Below is a table highlighting some meals that are high in carbohydrates.

Table 18: High-carbohydrate Meals

MEAL	CARBOHYDRATES (g)
Baked potato (medium) with beans	108
Wholewheat toast with jam (per slice)	25
Low-fat milk (1 pint)	23
Pasta (1 cup) with tomato sauce	88
Fruit (e.g. apple) and low-fat yoghurt (1 serving)	65
Cereal with chopped banana (1 serving)	61
Pizza base with tomato sauce and onions (medium)	49
Rice (1 cup) and vegetables (1 cup)	69
Fruit juice (1 pint)	58
Low-fat chips and beans (1 serving)	72

Consuming 700 g of carbohydrate is often easier said than done. In order to get your daily quota of carbohydrates you will need to consume a large volume of food. Indeed 700 g of carbohydrate is equivalent to six and a half servings of baked potato and baked beans. If this dietary protocol is too complicated or impractical for you a simple strategy is to consume 1 g/kg bodyweight of carbohydrate polymer (commercial carbohydrate powder) in addition to your regular meals twice per day for three days prior to the race.

In order to further maximise carbohydrate storage you should consume a carbohydrate-rich meal prior to the race. Sports scientists are in agreement that a meal containing approximately 250 to 300 g of carbohydrate should be taken three to four hours before the race. A typical pre-race meal could comprise a couple of baked potatoes with baked beans, a couple of bananas and a carbohydrate drink. The timing of this meal is not an exact science, as it is subject to the speed of your digestive system and how comfortable you feel. You may find that you can tolerate a pre-race meal later than recommended or, conversely, you may require a longer period of time to process the meal. Only time will tell, so experiment during your training rides rather than test it out at an important event.

It is common practice for some riders to snack on a carbohydrate-rich energy bar a few minutes before the start of the race; others drink a strong carbohydrate polymer solution (20 to 30 per cent). Again, the sports science jury is out on this because research findings are equivocal. Perhaps this is because riders vary in their response to pre-race feeding and, as with any nutritional plan, it is worth experimenting beforehand in order to find out what works for you.

Dietary Strategy during the Race

Almost immediately after you begin the race, your muscle glycogen stores are being heavily called upon to supply the fuel for muscular contraction. The inroad into your carbohydrate stores has begun and will continue until they are depleted. As this happens, there is an increasing reliance on blood glucose as the fuel source. Blood glucose levels need to be maintained and this is achieved in three ways:

1. The breakdown and discharge of muscle glycogen;
2. Synthesis of glucose from fat and protein (a process known as 'gluconeogenesis' which occurs in the liver);
3. From oral carbohydrate ingestion.

It is the latter that you have control over once the race has started, and your carbohydrate supplementation strategy during the race is just as important as any of the other race tactics you may have. For any mountain bike race or training session lasting longer than an hour, oral carbohydrate supplementation will be of benefit to you. It takes time for the carbohydrate to be absorbed, so you should start drinking your carbohydrate solution as early on in the race as possible. This will help conserve your glycogen stores and thus delay the onset of fatigue. As a rule of thumb, you should aim to consume about half a litre of a 15 per cent carbohydrate polymer solution (see energy drinks below) every hour. To remind yourself to drink frequently, set your watch alarm to go off every 15 minutes.

Post-race dietary strategy

Following a race or training session, as soon as you get off your bike, you should immediately be thinking about replacing your carbohydrate stores. This is because it can take up to two days for glycogen stores to reach pre-exercise levels based on a typical diet. As we have seen in earlier chapters, in order to maximise the effect of your training you need to exercise more than once every 48 hours. It is therefore imperative that you restock your glycogen stores as quickly as possible.

Following exercise there is a glycogen window, during which consumed carbohydrates are assimilated into glycogen at approximately three times the rate at resting levels. As a result of the previous exercise, your muscles are still primed for accumulating carbohydrates and they do so at a rapid rate. After a period of time these beneficial effects wear off and glycogen replenishment drops back to basal rates. Research suggests that this glycogen window is open for anywhere up to four hours post exercise, so in order to maximise its potential benefit you should start reloading your carbohydrates as soon as possible, preferably within the first 20 minutes. If the glycogen window is used to its maximum effect, the bulk of glycogen storage is complete within 24 hours. Because of this you are then ready to exercise the following day.

Diagram 18: The Effects of High- and Low-carbohydrate Diets and the Glycogen Window

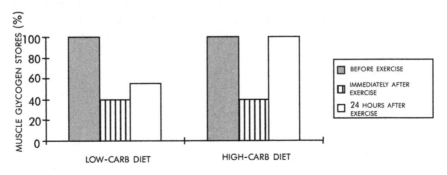

The diet following a race should be similar to that of beforehand: high in carbohydrates. In addition, contemporary research indicates that if the carbohydrates are taken in conjunction with protein then muscle glycogen re-synthesis is enhanced above the levels found when just consuming carbohydrate alone. To take advantage of this, you should add 0.5 g/kg bodyweight of protein powder (found in health food and bodybuilding shops) to the carbohydrate that you use to make up your energy drink.

ENERGY DRINKS

There is an ever-increasing number of commercially prepared energy drinks on the market, but beware: not all of them are equal. The osmotic potential of the drink is very important. Osmotic potential refers to the tendency of a solution to remove water from pure water by the process of osmosis through a cell membrane. The more molecules of glucose you add to water, the greater the osmotic potential of the solution. A solution which is low in osmotic activity (weak solution) is preferred because it can be emptied from the stomach at a quicker rate. Unfortunately glucose has a high osmotic potential and as such will empty from the stomach very slowly and will not be readily available for use. High concentrations of glucose (strong solution) may even draw water from the body into the stomach, thus contributing to dehydration, which can be dangerous in a hot environment.

Instead of drinking a glucose solution, it is advisable that you consume a glucose polymer drink (such as maltodextrin) which is less osmotically active. This is because there are relatively fewer particles in the solution. A glucose polymer consists of glucose units joined together and each polymer has different properties according to its size and structure. The structural information is usually written on the labels of the product and are usually expressed according to the percentage of polymers they contain as well as the average size of the polymer. The higher the value the better.

Mixing your Energy Drink

The role of the energy drink is twofold: firstly, to replace any fluid you have lost and thus prevent dehydration; and secondly, to match the energy expenditure of your mountain biking. Unfortunately, these two factors enjoy a negatively correlated relationship. In other words, depending upon how you mix your energy drink, you can either do one very well at the expense of the other, or do both but not at their maximum rate.

A great deal of scientific literature is devoted to unearthing an ideal carbohydrate solution that can deliver both water and carbohydrate at a high rate. The findings, like anything else nutritional, are generalisations and may not suit you without some modification. The starting recommendation is to consume about one gram of glucose polymer per kilogram of bodyweight per hour. If you add this to your standard drinks bottle then it works out at about a 12 to 15 per cent solution. If you increase this percentage, it will take longer for the solution to empty from your stomach. This may not be a bad thing on cold days, but when racing in the heat you will want to re-hydrate your body as quickly as possible to avoid dehydration. Under these conditions it is advisable to mix up a solution of 10 per cent or less (5 g carbohydrate powder to 500 ml of water).

WATER AND AVOIDING DEHYDRATION

Water is perhaps the most important sports drink of them all. Although it does not supply any of the energy needed for mountain biking, it does help prevent dehydration, which if left unchecked can be fatal.

The human body is basically a large leather bag filled with water. The average person contains a staggering 40 litres of water, which sounds a lot. Indeed, you may be forgiven for thinking that you can lose a fair amount of this water before there is a problem. However, this is not the case. It has been found that for every 1 per cent loss of bodyweight due to dehydration there is a 2 per cent reduction in performance, which in real terms is only a little over a drinks bottle's worth. At the other end of the scale, a loss of only 10 per cent means death is imminent. Dehydration is therefore a real threat to your mountain biking performance.

Most mountain bikers only reach for their water bottles when they get thirsty. However, don't rely solely on your body to tell you when you need a drink. Your thirst mechanism works on a negative-feedback loop. That is, you have to lose water before your thirst mechanism kicks in. By then it is too late, though, and your performance is already suffering.

The best way to stay hydrated when you are mountain biking is to drink 'little and often' whether you feel thirsty or not. The type of drink that you consume will also have a significant effect upon your hydration status. Avoid alcohol, coffee, tea, soft drinks or anything containing caffeine because they are diuretics and can actually cause you to lose water. The best drink for re-hydration is plain water. However, when you are mountain biking you will also want your drink to supply you with energy.

As mentioned previously, carbohydrate depletion is a major contributor to fatigue in a mountain bike race. The logical solution to this problem is to drink carbohydrate-rich drinks. This procedure, while increasing the amount of fuel available to the body, also decreases the rate of emptying from the stomach and ultimately decreases the rate at which it can be made available. On the other hand, a plain water drink is readily emptied from the stomach and available for absorption within 20 minutes. However, it does not supply any energy. Therefore a trade-off exists between supplying water and supplying carbohydrates. In making your decision, you must carefully assess the training or race conditions.

The environment in which you exercise will have a dramatic effect on your rate of fluid loss. Hot, humid environments will result in the greatest amount of fluid loss. Whilst mountain biking in the heat, it is not unusual to lose up to two litres of water every hour through sweating; this can mean it is impossible to replace water at the rate at which it is being lost, and as such a negative fluid balance will occur. In order to recover fully, this net reduction of body fluid needs replacing. To remedy this, weigh yourself before and after your ride and replace the difference in weight with the equivalent amount of water. For every kilogram of body weight lost, drink one litre of water.

It is also worth bearing in mind that dehydration due to sweating can even occur in cold environments. The problem arises if you wrap up warm when you are sedentary and then begin exercising. The heat produced as a result of the exercise cannot escape and you slowly start to overheat. Your body's response to this is to attempt to lose heat through sweating. It is therefore important to maximise the benefits of a layering system, removing and adding layers as appropriate. To exacerbate dehydration even further, an increased amount of water vapour is lost during respiration in a cold environment as opposed to a warmer one. To reduce the possibility of dehydration, you should always make a conscious effort to drink frequently.

Electrolytes which are essential for proper nerve and muscle function are also lost through sweating. However, a well balanced diet will replace any lost electrolytes (for example one banana will replace most of the missing potassium), but if you are prone to cramps, or intend spending long, consecutive days in the hills, there are plenty of commercial isotonic drinks which will replace these lost salts.

Tips for Avoiding Dehydration

1. Ensure you are fully hydrated before your training ride or race.

    This sounds like common sense but is often overlooked by many mountain bikers, especially prior to a race when their minds are often on a million and one other things. As a rule of thumb you should be able to urinate just before the start of the race and it should be clear.

2. Drink small volumes often, even if you don't feel thirsty.

    During a mountain bike race this is often overlooked, as there are many other things to contend with. To remind yourself to drink frequently set your watch alarm to go off every 15 minutes.

3. Replace lost water after the ride.

    It can often be difficult to replace all of the lost water during the training ride or race. As soon as possible afterwards, drink to replenish the lost water and restore your fluid levels (remember: difference in bodyweight, 1 kilogram = 1 litre).

4. Wear clothing which will not cause you to overheat.

It is very easy to wear clothing that will cause you to overheat, especially in cold climates. Maximise the use of a layering system, and as a rule of thumb err on the side of caution. Start your exercise off feeling slightly cold rather than warm.

5. Plan for fluid and energy replacement.

If both dehydration and glycogen depletion are expected, fit two bottles to your bike: one containing carbohydrate solution, the other plain water.

6. Experiment with glycerol.

Glycerol is an ergogenic aid that you may wish to try in order to help maintain your hydration status. Is does not work for everyone, so if you decide to use it experiment with it in your training rides. For further information on glycerol see chapter sixteen.

ENERGY BARS AND GELS

Energy bars and gels are carbohydrate-dense foods which are designed to supply energy during a race or training workout. Commercially available energy bars are ideal because they are compact, impact resistant, tasty and easily digestible. Some manufacturers also fortify their energy bars with vitamins, minerals and macro-nutrients, which also make them an ideal post-exercise recovery snack. The downside is they tend to be rather bland and expensive. However, it is possible to make your own energy bars which are cheap and contain your favourite ingredients.

Energy Bar Recipe

INGREDIENTS:

100 g dried fruit (e.g. 50 g dates, 50 g apricots)

50 g raisins

25 g brown sugar

35 g carbohydrate powder (maltodextrin)

80 g plain flour

60 g rice krispies

100 g runny honey

100 g golden syrup

50 g fruit spread

150 g oats

PREPARATION: Chop up the dried fruit.

COOKING: Place the dried fruit into a pan and add a little water. Simmer gently until the fruit is tender. Mix in the fruit spread, honey and syrup and gently heat until runny. Mix the remaining ingredients in a bowl and add the syrup/honey mix. Stir thoroughly. Pour into a greaseproof baking tin and place in a preheated oven for 30 minutes at 175 °C. Remove from oven, allow to cool and then cut into bars.

NUTRITIONAL INFORMATION: Each bar contains approximately:

Total Calories	213 kcal	
Carbohydrates	47.25 g	89% Calories
of which sugars	24.5 g	
Fat	1.2 g	5% Calories
of which saturates	0	
Protein	3.35 g	6% Calories
Cholesterol	0	
Sodium	40 mg	

THE BALANCED DIET

So far, we have looked at supplying the energy needed for mountain biking. However, this should not be the limit of your nutritional goals or knowledge. Fine, we have sorted out the training and racing diet, but we also need to consider the anabolic, catabolic and metabolic processes that occur during recovery and on a day-to-day basis.

Your body needs varying amounts of diverse nutrients. Each food comprises a different nutrient make-up, and in order to ensure that you consume them all, it is good practice to eat a varied diet. Nutrients are destroyed by cooking and processing and as such you should always try to ensure that your food is as close to its raw state as possible. The less processing the better.

Everybody has individual, nutritional needs depending upon various factors – such as age, gender, fitness status and illness, to name but a few – and a blueprint diet for everyone does not exist. However, the following table offers a guideline.

Table 19: Recommended Daily Servings of Foods:

FOODSTUFF	NUMBER OF SERVINGS
Fats, oils, sweets and desserts	As few as possible
Dairy products	2–3
Meat, poultry, eggs, fish and nuts	2–3
Fruit	2–4
Vegetables	4–5
Cereal, bread, rice	7–11
Water	unlimited

Fibre

The fibre or 'roughage' in your diet has no nutritional value. Instead it provides bulk and assists in keeping you regular. Too little can cause constipation, whereas too much may inhibit the absorption of some minerals.

Vitamins and Minerals

The majority of metabolic reactions and processes that occur within the human body require the presence of vitamins and minerals. If the appropriate vitamin or mineral is not present in your diet then the reaction will not occur and you will suffer. It is therefore of paramount importance that you consume your necessary quota of vitamins.

Some dieticians argue that there is no need for vitamin or mineral supplementation if the athlete is eating a well-balanced and varied diet, because all their nutritional needs are being met. Others say that athletes require far more vitamins and minerals than a sedentary person and if they were to obtain them purely from diet alone then they would have to consume huge, impractical amounts of food to meet their needs. They therefore advocate the use of vitamin and mineral supplementation. Once again, it is a highly individual matter and the choice is yours.

A lot of riders take a daily multi-vitamin and mineral tablet as an 'insurance policy' against any deficiencies. On the whole this is not a bad practice, but care must be taken. Some vitamins, namely vitamins A,D, E and K are fat soluble and are stored. If these vitamins get consumed in mega doses then they can reach toxic levels and cause severe illness. The other vitamins, namely C and B, are water soluble and will be excreted as expensive urine. This latter group of vitamins can still build up to toxic levels if taken in extremely high dosages, so take care.

One thing is for sure: dieticians and nutritionists agree that vitamin and mineral supplements should supplement your diet and not replace parts of it. A poor diet can not be made to be a good one by popping a pill. If you consume high amounts of saturated fat in your diet, a pill will not make this any better. Instead, you should eat properly and if you so wish enhance your eating with a careful supplementation programme.

BODYWEIGHT MANAGEMENT

Bodyweight is often an important issue for both the competitive mountain biker and the fitness biker alike. Often the fitness biker is using mountain biking as a means to lose or maintain bodyweight, whereas the competitive mountain biker is chiefly concerned about race performance. The inverse relationship between bodyweight and performance is well documented and can affect the race outcome, especially in the cross-country discipline where riders must lift their bodyweight up hills against gravity. This is borne out by the current crop of elite-level cross-country riders who are typically very lean.

For health reasons your bodyweight should not fluctuate widely during the year. You should avoid rapid weight loss, as it places strain on your immune system and renders you susceptible to illness. A more realistic figure is to only allow a discrepancy of between 2 and 5 kg between your winter weight and your race weight. When reducing your bodyweight you should plan ahead, aiming to lose about half a kilogram per week. If you are a competitive mountain biker you may not have to make any special adjustments because the P2 phase usually initiates weight loss as a result of the increased workload.

Whatever your reason for weight loss the theory behind it is the same: you will lose weight if you consume fewer Calories than you use, and you will gain weight if the opposite is true.

A Few Fact and Figures

A kilogram of fat contains 1,590 kcal and mountain biking at an average speed of 9–10 mph off-road burns about 10 kcal every minute. So if you mountain bike for two and a half hours each week, you will expend 1,500 kcal (2.5 x 60 x 10 = 1,500) or the equivalent of about 1 kg of fat. Put another way, if you didn't mountain bike you would put on that extra kilogram of fat.

What Should I Do?

There are three possible ways to reduce bodyweight: consume less energy, expend more energy, or both. Crash dieting and all-out intense exercise regimes do not cause you to lose weight in the long term. It's a fact. The best way is to make little changes to your riding and dietary habits. Before eating, ask yourself whether you're eating it because you're hungry or just for the sake of it. If it's the latter, just have a small portion, or better still none at all. The secret is not to deny yourself the foods you like (which are often the most fattening), just cut down on them slightly. Over time these little calorie savings will add up and your bodyweight will go down.

You will also need to expend more energy, but there is a grey area in the literature as to the optimum nature of exercise to promote weight loss. Some scientists are in favour of long, slow rides because the majority of energy supplied for such exercise comes predominantly from fat stores. However, more recent evidence has shown that it is simply the balance between total Calories eaten and those expended (whatever the source: carbohydrates, fats, or protein) that determines whether weight is gained or lost. Either way you will need to get out on your mountain bike more.

Tips for Weight Control

1. Avoid food that is high in fat. Not only is this approach good for your heart, but it also reduces the number of Calories that you consume. Remember that weight for weight, fat contains over double the amount of Calories that carbohydrates and protein do.

2. Maintain a high percentage of dietary carbohydrates. If you keep your Calorie intake of carbohydrates between 55 and 60 per cent, your overall Calorie intake will be reduced

3. Avoid missing breakfast. You should make a concerted effort to have breakfast every morning. Eating breakfast restores your glycogen and blood glucose levels and prevents you having to snack mid-morning. If on occasion you are pushed for time the ultimate quick breakfast is a glass of skimmed milk and a glass of orange juice.

4. Eat fruit as snacks. If you need to snack between meals, try having fruit. In addition to satiating your hunger, you will be taking on board valuable nutrients.

5. Avoid eating before going to bed. Eat your last meal several (at least two) hours before you go to bed. Research indicates that meals taken just before going asleep are converted to fat more quickly than if they had been eaten earlier.

16. ERGOGENIC AIDS

Athletes the world over are seemingly so desperate to improve their sporting performance that, in order to gain the advantage over their competitors, they will put their faith and trust in powders, pills, and potions, which have apparent miraculous properties. This may mean, for certain athletes, the use of illegal drugs. However, millions of pounds each year are spent on ergogenic aids such as creatine monohydrate, bee pollen and herbal teas, which at the time of writing are not illegal either under civil law or sports federation rules.

It is beyond the scope of this book to give an exhaustive account of all the ergogenic aids available to the competitive mountain biker. Instead, in this chapter I shall review the most widely used ergogenic aids in competitive mountain biking.

CAFFEINE

Caffeine is synonymous with coffee, and anybody who is not a 'morning person' will no doubt have experienced the beneficial effects that coffee has. However caffeine is not only present in coffee but also in a wide range of other readily available foodstuffs including chocolate, tea and cola, as well as being available pure in tablet form.

Many competitive mountain bikers also enjoy the pick-me-up effects of caffeine and use it to their advantage in races. Recent, well-controlled studies have shown that when performing an endurance cycling test to exhaustion, riders who had consumed caffeine prior to the test were able to cycle for longer than those who had not. One of the theories behind this is that caffeine may have a glycogen-sparing effect by readily mobilising free fatty acids for use as an energy substrate, thus delaying the onset of fatigue.

It seems that downhill mountain bikers may benefit from caffeine ingestion as well, because it appears to enhance short-term intense cycling that lasts around five minutes. This may be due to caffeine affecting the contractions of the exercising muscles.

Caffeine is a restricted or controlled substance in the eyes of the Sports Council and excessive use of it may result in a positive urine test if you are involved in British Cycling Federation competitions. Riders are allowed up to 12 micrograms of caffeine per ml urine before it is considered illegal, however it is not easy to reach that limit by drinking coffee alone, as an average[1] rider would have to drink about six or eight cups of percolated coffee one hour before the race for the test to register anywhere near positive. To date, most positive tests have involved riders that have used caffeine tablets.

Reports have indicated that moderate caffeine consumption of 5 mg of caffeine per kg of bodyweight one hour prior to exercise has a beneficial effect on cycling performance to exhaustion. For a 70 kg rider, this equates to approximately 3½ cups of instant coffee taken one hour before the race.

Table 20: Caffeine Content of Typical Beverages

DRINK	CAFFEINE CONTENT (mg)
Coffee	
Drip method (1 cup)	100–150
Percolated (1 cup)	65–125
Instant (1 cup)	40–110
Tea (1 cup = 150 ml)	30–50
Cola (can 330 ml)	35–50

As a rule of thumb, a cup of coffee which contains 100 mg of caffeine will give a urine reading of approximately 1.50 micrograms of caffeine per ml urine and a can of cola will give a urine reading of approximately 0.70 micrograms of caffeine per ml urine.

The effects of caffeine diminish with continued use. In a way your body gets used to it and you have to take a greater amount to get the same desired effect. It is therefore wise to have a coffee-free period, of about a week, immediately prior to the race, and then take the appropriate amount of coffee an hour before the race. Caffeine has a diuretic effect, so you should take extra care in ensuring that you are fully hydrated prior to, and during, the race.

Besides staying within 'legal' limits there are a number of other issues you must carefully consider before using caffeine as an ergogenic aid. Riders who have ingested large quantities of caffeine have reported various side effects including dizziness, insomnia, irritability and gastrointestinal distress. These side effects only tend to be apparent when riders have used high dosages (9 mg caffeine per kg of body weight) and do not appear to be a problem with moderate caffeine usage

---

[1] Different people respond in different ways. If in doubt, have a caffeine tolerance test.

(3–5 mg per kg of bodyweight). Coffee has been shown to inhibit the absorption of thiamine (essential for carbohydrate metabolism) as well as calcium and iron. It is therefore wise to ensure that you have an adequate amount of these nutrients in your diet and that you have coffee-free periods.

CREATINE

Creatine supplementation is a relative newcomer to the world of sports nutrition. It enjoyed a meteoric rise to fame in the 1980s when many World class sprinters accredited their performance to its use. In chapter one we looked at the phosphocreatine energy system and the role it plays in adenosine triphosphate (ATP) resynthesis. The basic premise behind creatine supplementation is to maximise the muscles' store of creatine so that ATP regeneration will be optimised. Because of the nature of the energy system creatine interacts with, its ergogenic properties are ideally suited to sports which require fast, explosive, repeated bursts of energy, of which downhill mountain biking is a prime example.

In addition to supplying instantaneous energy, creatine phosphate has been found to act as a buffer which helps control spikes in muscle acidity during intense exercise. Hydrogen ions, released from lactic acid formation during intense activity, are absorbed when creatine phosphate is broken down to resynthesise ATP. This prevents a build-up of hydrogen ions which interfere with the muscle contraction process and cause fatigue. This buffering action allows the muscle to work at high intensities for longer periods. Contemporary research is pointing to the supposition that creatine monohydrate supplementation can raise your anaerobic threshold as well. The exact mechanisms behind this are not, as yet, fully understood. It is believed that, because muscle fibre contraction is enhanced, fewer fibres are recruited in order to maintain a specific speed. If this is the case, the extrapolated thinking leads to the logical inference that less lactic acid is produced. As a result, creatine supplementation may have important ramifications for the cross-country racer.

Creatine is available in three forms: creatine phosphate, creatine citrate and creatine monohydrate. For oral supplementation, creatine monohydrate has been found to give the best ergogenic results. Some researchers suggest that taking creatine monohydrate with carbohydrates will further enhance its potency. Traditionally studies have had a five-day loading procedure of 20 g per day, followed by a maintenance phase of lower doses. As more research is performed, this method of loading is being questioned and the school of thought is now towards more moderate, lower doses.

Across the board, most studies have reported an increase in bodyweight as a result of water retention due to creatine supplementation. Whilst this had no adverse effect on the cycling performance experiments, it should be noted that the subjects were tested on stationary ergometers and as such did not have to move their bodyweight. In a mountain bike race scenario this may have a retarding effect on performance because the excess baggage will have to be carried throughout the race. That said, it is purported that the new moderate loading procedure does not have such significant effects on bodyweight.

There are still a lot of facts to be unearthed about creatine supplementation. The general consensus from sports scientists working in this field is that creatine supplementation has no adverse side effects on the health of users.

SODIUM BICARBONATE

Sodium bicarbonate is more commonly known as baking soda, or as Alka Seltzer if you suffer from hangovers! Its ergogenic benefits are observed during high-intensity sprints that last anywhere between one and six minutes. Outside this range, sodium bicarbonate is reported to have little observed effect. It is therefore most applicable to those riders involved in the downhill discipline.

Sodium bicarbonate buffers lactic acid, thus prolonging the duration of the sprint. Research has shown that the ideal dosage should be 300 mg per kg of bodyweight. Side effects associated with sodium bicarbonate ingestion include a bloated feeling, stomach upset and diarrhoea.

GLYCEROL

In chapter fifteen we examined the role of water in your diet, with the debilitating effects that dehydration can have on your mountain bike performance. With this in mind, recent research has found that glycerol supplementation, when accompanied by appropriate amounts of water intake, may help enhance performance by preventing dehydration.

Glycerol is a sweet-tasting chemical substance that has water-retaining properties and is used by athletes in a process called 'water loading'. In theory, following digestion, glycerol remains in the blood for some time. Whilst there, it draws water into the blood, thus maximising the hydration levels and the thermo-regulatory properties of the blood. Carefully controlled studies have reported 22 per cent increases in endurance for cyclists using a glycerol water mix before exercise, compared to a similar amount of plain water. Conversely other studies have found no significant difference between water/glycerol solutions and plain water.

There are several reported cases where subjects have suffered from headaches following glycerol ingestion. In addition others have reported feeling nauseated, bloated and light-headed – none of which are conducive to good mountain bike performance.

Without a doubt proper hydration is an important aspect of your mountain bike race preparation and a state of dehydration should be avoided at all times. The present research is equivocal regarding glycerol supplementation as an ergogenic aid. At the moment, the side effects overshadow the benefits and its advantages over plain water are not overwhelming.

17. YOUR FIRST RACE

RACE CATEGORIES

The previous chapters have been devoted to getting you 'mountain bike fit'. There is, of course, a lot of pleasure and satisfaction to be gleaned from the achievement of this goal. However, there is no better way to enjoy your hard-earned fitness than in the cut and thrust of a mountain bike race.

Races are held most weekends across the length and breadth of the country and the main races are advertised in the calendar section of the leading mountain bike magazines. The calendars are often sub-divided into the different types of racing and then divided further by date or geographical area. In addition, your local bike shop is often a good source of race information and can offer invaluable local-knowledge advice about the racecourse and the conditions. In order to ensure that your first experience of racing is a good one, it is important to select the appropriate category and race within your limitations. Most races are split into the categories shown below.

Table 21: Race Categories

CATEGORY	AGE	CATEGORY	AGE
Pee Wee	9 and under	Expert	19 and above
Sprogs	11 and under	Masters	30 to 40
Juveniles	12 to 13	Vets	40 and above
Youth	14 to 15	Grand Vets	50 and above
Junior	16 to 18	Fun	open to all
Sport	19 and above	Pro/Elite	n/a

With the exception of the large race meetings, very few will have all of the above categories. The number of categories is often depicted by the number of entries in the event and any permutation of the above can be possible. For first-time racers it is advisable to select the easiest race in the appropriate age category. Failing this, opt for the Fun category, which it must be said is often more competitive than the name suggests.

There is no hard-and-fast rule about how long a course should be. This is usually dictated by the geography of the venue. One lap can range from 2 to 10 miles and the number of laps is at the discretion of the race organiser. Some general guidelines exist for the winning time in each category and these are shown below. In order to meet these guidelines, the number of laps of a particular course will depend upon the course length.

Table 22: Winning Times

CATEGORY	MALES	FEMALES
Pee Wee	< 30 mins	< 30 mins
Sprogs	30 mins	30 mins
Juveniles	30 mins	30 mins
Youth	1 hr	30 mins
Junior	1 hr 30 mins	1 hr
Fun	1 hr	30 mins
Sport	1 hr 30 mins	1 hr
Expert	2 hrs	1 hr 30 mins
Masters	1 hr 30 mins	1 hr
Vets	1 hr 30 mins	1 hr
Grand Vets	1 hr	30 mins
Pro/Elite	2 hrs 30	1 hr 45 mins

For downhill, the length of the course is depicted by the terrain and can range from a couple of minutes in Britain to double figures in other parts of Europe and America.

ON THE DAY

To ensure that your first race goes smoothly and relatively hassle-free, you should arrive early (preferably the day before) and be prepared for every eventuality. Arriving early means that you can avoid the registration queues and have plenty of time to pre-ride the course and work out the best lines to take. It also allows you the time to make any final adjustments to your bike, or make the repairs that for some reason always need doing on race day!

What to take

Below is a checklist for what you should have in your kit bag:

- Helmet, shorts, race jersey, gloves, socks, shoes, shades, tights and long-sleeve jersey (if winter)
- Race food, drinks bottle
- Towel
- Warm clothing for afterwards
- Food and water for afterwards
- Choice of tyres
- Spare inner-tubes (you can never have too many)
- Tool kit
- Spare chain, gear and brake cable
- Chain lube
- Track pump
- First aid kit

The Philosophy

Whether your race début is cross-country, downhill, or dual slalom, you should view it as a hard training ride. That is all it is. Let the competition and the course test your mettle and enjoy being pushed further, but don't get hung up on winning first time out. Nor should you lament if you perform badly. Don't be afraid to make mistakes – no one will laugh at you if you pick the wrong line or have to push your bike up a climb. In fact you will learn more from your mistakes than you ever will do on the podium. Of course it is the podium where we all want to stand, but very few people have done it first time out. Serve your apprenticeship initially and then, when you can consistently finish in the top 20 of your category, set your sights higher and move up through the ranks.

Good luck!

GLOSSARY

AEROBIC The term applied to exercise or metabolic processes that require the presence of oxygen. Compare with anaerobic.

AGONIST The primary muscle which causes the movement in an exercise.

ANAEROBIC The term applied to exercise or metabolic processes that do not require the presence of oxygen. Compare with aerobic.

ANAEROBIC THRESHOLD The point where the aerobic energy system fails to meet the majority of energy demands of the body. As exercise activity increases beyond this threshold, more reliance is placed upon the anaerobic system to meet the energy demands.

ANTAGONIST The muscle that opposes the agonist is called the antagonist.

BONK The term associated with hypoglycaemia.

CAFFEINE A stimulant often used by sportspeople as an ergogenic aid. Found in coffee, tea and cola drinks, it is a controlled substance in the eyes of the British Cycling Federation.

CALLISTHENICS Exercises which are used to tone and strengthen muscles with the minimum of equipment. Bodyweight supplies the required resistance.

CARBOHYDRATE LOADING The process whereby glycogen stores are enhanced via dietary manipulation.

CARBOHYDRATES The most important fuel type for the competitive mountain biker. They should make up the bulk of your diet and contribute around 60 per cent of your total Calorie intake. See monosaccharides, disaccharides and polysaccharides.

CARDIO-RESPIRATORY SYSTEM The interaction of the cardiovascular system and the lungs. Compare with cardiovascular system.

CARDIOVASCULAR SYSTEM The system that contains the heart, blood vessels and the blood. Compare with cardio-respiratory system.

COOL-DOWN The process when a rider gradually tapers the intensity of the exercise following a training bout. Cool-downs have been shown to facilitate the recovery process.

CRAMP A painful, uncontrolled muscle contraction.

CREATINE An energy rich compound that is often used as an ergogenic aid. It is purported to enhance explosive activities such as sprinting and at time of writing is not a banned substance.

CROSS-COUNTRY A mountain bike discipline where competitors race against each other on an off-road course. These races last for an hour upwards.

CROSS-TRAINING A programme comprising different sports.

DIGESTION The process whereby food is broken down into its constituent parts by mechanical and chemical means.

DISACCHARIDES Double sugar units, formed when two monosaccharides are joined together. Compare with monosaccharides and polysaccharides.

DOWNHILL A mountain bike discipline where competitors aim to complete a downhill course in the quickest possible time.

DURATION The length of time of a workout.

ECHINACEA A common herb that is believed to boost the immune system.

ELECTROLYTES Salts, typically sodium, potassium and chloride, that are required for proper nerve transmission and muscular contraction.

ENDURANCE The ability to resist fatigue.

ENERGY BARS A convenient form of fuel for mountain bikers. They are carbohydrate dense and are useful for supplying energy during training or competition.

ENERGY DRINKS Drinks that typically contain glucose or glucose polymers. They are used by mountain bikers to replace energy, or act as an energy supplement during training or racing.

ERGOGENIC AID Anything that enhances athletic performance.

FAT A dietary component that should contribute 20 to 30 per cent of your total Calorie consumption. See monosaturated fats, polyunsaturated fats, saturated fats and trans fats.

FATIGUE Exhaustion of a muscle to the point where it can no longer work at the desired level.

FLEXIBILITY The range of movement at a joint.

FOUNDATION PHASE The first phase of a macrocycle during which basic fitness is developed.

FREQUENCY The number of workouts per week.

GLUCOSE A monosaccharide.

GLYCEROL An ergogenic that is purported to enhance performance by reducing the likelihood of dehydration.

GLYCOGEN The stored form of glucose. It is stored in the skeletal muscle and liver.

HAMSTRINGS The large muscle group on the back of the thigh.

HEART RATE The number of times the heart beats in one minute. The units are beats per minute (bpm).

HEART-RATE MONITOR A device used to measure the heart rate of a rider.

HYPOGLYCAEMIA A condition occurring when there is a low blood glucose concentration. It is associated with feeling weak, confused, irritable and uncoordinated.

INTENSITY A measure of how hard the exercise is. Usually expressed in terms of heart rate, speed, strength, time, or power.

INTERVAL TRAINING A form of exercise during which intense exercise bouts are punctuated by relief periods.

LACTIC ACID The by-product of anaerobic exercise.

MACROCYCLE The length of the training programme.

MESOCYCLE A subdivision of a macrocycle. Each mesocycle typically has a different focus.

METABOLIC RATE The total amount of energy expended by an individual.

MICROCYCLE The smallest subdivision of a macrocycle. It typically lasts one week.

MONOSACCHARIDES Single sugar units which are the basic components of any carbohydrate. Glucose and fructose are the most common dietary monosaccharides. Compare with disaccharides and polysaccharides.

MONOUNSATURATED FATS Mainly vegetable oils, the most common being olive oil. Compare with saturated fats and polyunsaturated fats.

MUSCULAR ENDURANCE The ability of a muscle to contract repeatedly without fatiguing.

OVERLOAD A training load that is greater than that to which the body is accustomed.

OVER-TRAINING A state of extreme mental and physical fatigue.

PEAK PHASE A period of training where all fitness components are at their optimum. This usually coincides with the race season.

PEAK PREPARATION PHASE Occurs prior to the peak phase. During this phase training becomes more sports specific.

PERIODISATION The structure and organisation of a training programme in order to achieve a goal.

PLYOMETRICS A form of training in which a muscle is stretched prior to contraction.

POLYSACCHARIDES Long chains of monosaccharides combined together. Compare with monosaccharides and disaccharides.

POLYUNSATURATED FATS The least harmful of all dietary fats. They actually increase the levels of high-density lipoprotein (HDL) and reduce the level of low-density lipoprotein (LDL). Compare with monounsaturated fats and saturated fats.

POWER A function of strength and speed.

PROGRESSIVE OVERLOAD The method of continuously increasing the workload in order to maintain adaptation.

PROTEINS Made up from amino acids, they should contribute between 15 and 20 per cent of the Calories from your diet. The main roles of protein within the human body are growth, repair and homeostasis.

QUADRICEPS A large muscle group on the front of the thigh.

RECOVERY The time following training when restoration to pre-exercise condition occurs.

REPETITION The number of times an exercise is performed within a set.

RESISTANCE TRAINER A training device that enables cycle training to be performed indoors.

REVERSIBILITY A return to pre-training fitness levels as a result of inactivity.

SATURATED FATS Mainly found in animal fats and dairy products and typically solid at room temperature. Saturated fats are linked to heart disease because they increase the levels of LDL and contribute to atherosclerosis of the arteries and arteriosclerosis. Compare with monounsaturated fats and polyunsaturated fats.

SET The total number of continuous repetitions of an exercise.

SPECIFICITY A principle of training based on specific exercises initiating specific training responses.

SPEED The measurement of how fast you can cover a specific distance.

STRENGTH The ability to apply a force against a resistance.

SUPERCOMPENSATION A state when the adaptive responses to exercise are higher than normal levels.

TAPERING A reduction in training volume prior to a race. Usually used in conjunction with carbohydrate loading.

TRACK STAND A skill where the rider and bike remain stationary with only the tyres in contact with the ground.

TRAINING CAMP A period of time (usually two weeks) when a rider focuses solely on their fitness training. Training camps are usually based abroad and coincide with the UK's colder months.

TRAINING TAPER The reduction of training volume, usually in preparation for a competition.

TRAINING VOLUME The total amount of training performed in a specific time frame. It is a function of exercise intensity, duration and frequency.

TRAINING ZONE A reference to the heart-rate limits that correspond to a training intensity. Specific training zones elicit specific training responses.

TRANS FATS Man-made fats, the product of hydrogenating unsaturated fats. Unfortunately, this process makes the trans fat behave like a saturated fat and they cause the levels of LDL to rise. A major dietary source of trans fats are biscuits.

TURBO TRAINER A training device that enables cycle training to be performed indoors.

VO$_2$ MAX The maximum volume of oxygen that a body can absorb and utilise.

WARM-UP The procedure a rider performs prior to a competition or training in order to prepare, both physically and mentally, for the upcoming exercise.

WASTE PRODUCTS The by-products of metabolism, removed from the body. Typically they are toxic and, if left to accumulate in the body, they can become harmful.

WORLD CHAMPIONSHIPS A one-race event where the outright winner is crowned the World Champion.

WORLD CUP A series of races that lasts for the duration of the season. Riders accumulate points according to how they place in individual races. At the end of the series the competitors are ranked according to their cumulative points.